Few people have the guts to say the things that Terri has written in this book. Timely for every Christian seeking to be used by God as a leader, *A Servant of the Lord* is a manual for overcoming obstacles that keep us from growing. Whether a seasoned leader or not, every Christ follower will find the words of this book inspiring and challenging to their faith.

Pastor Mark Canfield
Lead Pastor
Pinellas Community Church
St. Petersburg, Florida

A Servant of the Lord

A SERVANT OF THE LORD

TERRI DIETER

A STRANG COMPANY

A Servant of the Lord by Terri Dieter
Published by Creation House
A Strang Company
600 Rinehart Road
Lake Mary, Florida 32746
www.creationhouse.com

Terri Dieter's photo courtesy of Tim Salmonson

Cover design by Terry Clifton

Library of Congress Control Number: 2007924898
International Standard Book Number: 978-1-59979-189-0

First Edition

07 08 09 10 11 — 987654321
Printed in the United States of America

My child, don't lose sight of good planning and insight. Hang on to them, for they fill you with life and bring you honor and respect. They keep you safe on your way and keep your feet from stumbling. You can lie down without fear and enjoy pleasant dreams. You need not be afraid of disaster or the destruction that comes upon the wicked, for the LORD is your security. He will keep your foot from being caught in a trap.

—PROVERBS 3:21–26

For every heart that beats with a passion to serve the Lord, for every ear that longs to hear "well done," for every eye looking toward the coming of His kingdom, and for every hand that aches to touch and see set free those who are lost, blind, bound, broken hearted, and bruised. This book is for you.

ACKNOWLEDGMENTS

ALTHOUGH THERE HAVE been many men and women used of the Lord to nurture, train, and teach me, I would like to say a special thank you to some special men chosen to be the Lord's developing hand in my life.

To Rip Waters, a special person chosen of the Lord to teach me the power of delegated authority and how to walk in it. Rip, your uncompromising command and absolute commitment to excellence were great sources of instruction and training. You were handpicked by the Lord to show me the responsibility one can shoulder when authority is delegated. I will forever be grateful.

To my earthly father, Donald Coffman, who loved me and modeled for me godly integrity, forthrightness, diligence, and loyalty. Dad, your unyielding standards are a testimony to the power of covenant commitment. You are a wonderful daddy, and I love you very much.

To Joe VanKoevering, whose God-given teaching gift was chosen of the Lord to lay the Word of God in my heart, line upon line, and precept upon precept. The Lord gave me His best. Through you an ark was constructed in my heart that brought me safely through many storms.

To Billy Burke, a special person who kept watch of my soul for ten years. You were the hand of the Lord to feed me, prune me, stretch me, break me, and mend me. As you were faithful to Him, He was faithful to me, and through you, He watered the good seed and pulled the tares. It was not always comfortable, but it was always ultimately wonderful. I love you, Billy, and I count it a great honor to have been chosen by the Lord to be one of your assignments. *Thank you* falls way short of what rests within my heart.

To David Melendez, whose leadership placed God's thumbprint on my heart. Thank you, David, for broadening my scope, enlarging my tents, and elevating my vantage point. My love and respect for you and who you are in Him runs deep.

To Mark Canfield, my wonderful pastor. Your patience, covenant love, godly leadership, and spiritual wholeness were used of the Lord to bring healing and liberty to this bruised and wounded servant. It is my joy to know you! It is my honor to serve you! It is my privilege to call you *friend*!

To my wonderful husband, Steve, who for all our years has loved me, encouraged me, and supported my pursuit to know my God. Never once did you complain, and with each opportunity chose to release me to do all that was in my heart to do. Your love, patience, loyalty, and pure heart were a gift to me and must truly bless our Lord's heart. I love you!

To my beloved Stephen-Paul, whose love for the Lord and love for his parents blesses me in a way no words can touch. Your light is so bright; your heart so pure! You are the kindest and most genuine human being I have ever known, and you have enriched my life beyond words. I watch with great anticipation to see how the Lord will continue to bless this world through you. I didn't deserve you, but I am so grateful the Lord allowed me to be your mother. I love you, my son!

Above all, to my precious heavenly Father, who loved me when I ran from Him, accepted me when I rejected Him, took me in when I was broken, set my wing, and not only taught me to fly again, but to fly higher for Him. I love you, Lord, with all my heart and with all my soul. With all that is within me, I bless your holy name!

CONTENTS

FOREWORD

EARLY ONE MORNING I was awakened from a dream.

The dream took place where I live—on an island off the gulf coast of Florida. While standing in my front yard my attention was drawn to water lapping over the tops of my feet, much like standing by the seashore. At first I thought the water was coming from our sprinkler system. I later realized, as I lifted my sights, that there was too much water for it to be coming from the sprinklers. I looked toward the street and noticed the water was much deeper, coming in again as shallow waves. With water now above my ankles, I lifted my sights higher to across the street. There were three- to five-foot waves breaking around the houses. As I looked beyond the houses, I saw large, fifteen- to twenty-foot waves crashing into the center of the island. Immediately, I ran into our house, warned my family, and looked out a window to the parking lot across the street. There were numerous red emergency rescue trucks covering the parking lot. Red lights were flashing and announcements were being made over loud speakers. The message was, "There is no reason to panic. Stay calm. Everything will be OK, and when this is all over, everyone will know the truth." I woke up.

I began to seek the Lord concerning the dream. My initial assumption was that the Lord was warning our family of a coming hurricane or tidal wave. However, as I continued to seek Him, I recorded the following in my personal journal:

There is a move coming, a wave coming,
That will deliver My people and crush their enemies.
The same wave will be deliverance to those who love Me
And judgment to those who do not.

It is to be feared by those who do not know Me
And welcomed by those who do.
When it has passed, all will know the truth.

Be not afraid of My judgment,
But anticipate its coming.
Be strong and trust in Me.
Love not your life unto death.
Do not seek to save your life,
For that is when you will lose it.

It was then that I realized the time had finally come for me to pen what the Lord placed in my heart concerning His servants.

INTRODUCTION

THE TIME IS late and the hour is near when all we have been prepared to do, all we have been destined to be, will be called upon. There is a quietness in the heavens shouting to my ears as if all of heaven is standing at attention, awaiting the trumpet sound. Whatever preparation has not been done must be done quickly before we are to be called forth. For the Lord promised to pour out His Spirit on all flesh, not just prepared and ready flesh. At that time, whatever has been crucified will receive of His Spirit; whatever has not will be exposed.

Ready or not, I believe He is soon to manifest His glory at levels rarely experienced in times past. We must undertake whatever final preparation is needed, trusting that He will complete His work *in us*. Our surrender to His workings will determine the extent to which He will complete His work *through us*. We must not only be *called*; we must be chosen. We must not only be chosen; we must answer that call with obedience.

This is a book about destiny. This is a book about God's chosen vessels. This is a book I believe reveals the heart of the Father relative to His end-time warriors. I fervently pray the words to follow will minister life to your spirit and that your discernment will be sharp, insuring you take into *your spirit* only that which is of *His Spirit*. I am but a human vessel desiring the message placed in my heart to come forth with purity. Only by His divine grace can that be accomplished.

This is not intended to be a feel-good book. It rather may be a book you must endure to the end. I believe, however, that if you will commit to endure, you will find yourself at a crossroad where the choice is clear and the path is bright. This is not a drop of medicine placed in a spoonful of honey. This is the medicine at full strength. Hold your nose, swallow quickly, do whatever you have to do, but I beseech you to take it and swallow it. There is no time for coaxing and pampering. The Word of God is sharp. It will sometimes cut. Know that it will only cut away that which will hinder you. Remember it is because of His awesome love for us that He brings discipline to our lives.

While this is a book that can be read by any believer and impart truths that will dramatically escalate their maturity, I have come to realize this is a book designed for leadership. Touch a believer with the yoke-destroying truths of God's heart and mind, and you have blessed a believer. Touch a leader, and you have blessed all those who are under their care and watch. The unlimited power that results from corporate agreement, submission, and obedience to the Lord produces the powerful force of unity that will be the bride Jesus awaits to present to the world.

The message in this book is not for others; it is for you. Let it touch you; let it change you; let it encourage you; and by the fruits in your life it will touch, change, and encourage those around you! We can teach what we know, but by His Spirit, we can also impart to others the very life He has put in us.

My prayer is for you to come away from this book prepared, purposed, focused, and aimed to fulfill your God-ordained destiny on this earth, for such a time as this, to the glory of our precious Lord and Savior, Jesus Christ.

Chapter 1

DESTINY CALLS

> Therefore, since we are surrounded by such a huge crowd of witnesses to the life of faith, let us strip off every weight that slows us down, especially the sin that so easily hinders our progress. And let us run with endurance the race that God has set before us. We do this by keeping our eyes on Jesus, on whom our faith depends from start to finish. He was willing to die a shameful death on the cross because of the joy he knew would be his afterward. Now he is seated in the place of highest honor beside God's throne in heaven.
>
> —Hebrews 12:1–2

There is within the heart of every believer a desire to be used of the Lord, to walk in the destiny to which He has called them, and to make a difference in the lives of others. The Lord Himself placed this desire in our hearts. Unfortunately the pursuit of this goal too often produces years of frustration, disappointment, and what sometimes seem to be never-ending cycles of repeated experiences. This, in large part, is due to stumbling blocks being placed in our path that are designed to sidetrack or stop our forward advancement. The bad news is these stumbling blocks are placed there by the enemy, but the good news is they are allowed there by the Lord to qualify His overcomers.

As believers, we are called to be a mighty army prepared for battle. To achieve this, these stumbling blocks must be overcome, because they will not go away. The question is not whether the Lord will have an army. The question is, Will you be prepared for the call when it is time to be chosen for that army? The Lord tells us that "many are called, but few are chosen" (Matt. 22:14). Do you want to be in that few? As part of our inheritance, we are all called. The Lord has provided for us a spiritual uniform; it is hanging in our spiritual closets. He once showed me my uniform. I remember noticing the tailored and slim design. It was regal and impressive. Right then it hit me, if I were to be called forth that day I would not be chosen because I could not fit into my uniform. There was too much of *me*! That realization struck a chord in my spirit, and from that day to this I have endeavored to become prepared by Him for my assignment.

If He were to call you today, would you fit into your uniform? When the trumpet blows, will you be ready and prepared to respond? Have you allowed Him to remove the parts that would be a hindrance? I am not referring to your natural size but rather your spiritual fitness. Would you fit into your spiritual uniform today? Are you ready? He has asked me to tell you that you can be ready; He wants you to be; and He has a tailored plan of preparation to insure you are.

If your answer is yes, then no matter what position you now hold within the body of Christ, this writing is given to you for a threefold purpose:

First, I hope to help you recognize those external hindrances designed to take you off course, trip you up, or stop you altogether from fulfilling your God-ordained calling. External hindrances are strategically planned to stop your advancement and alter your course. Your adversary does not care which course you take, just so it is not the course you are destined to take. For it is in being obedient to your calling that you will be most beneficial to the kingdom of God and at the same time do the most damage to the kingdom of darkness.

My second reason for writing this book is to identify those internal hindrances the Lord desires to remove. They are the areas of your personality and nature that are not yielded to the Lord and are therefore the areas keeping your spiritual uniform from fitting. External hindrances will take you off course if they can network with an internal hindrance you have not allowed to be removed by the grace of God.

The third reason I wrote this is to place before you the choice of being a bond slave of Christ. A bond slave is a slave by choice; their free will is never violated. Only in this place of servanthood and covenant commitment can we walk in the destiny we are called by Jesus to fulfill.

Stumbling blocks that are exposed to truth will be overcome. If we can be destroyed for a lack of knowledge, how much greater can deception be destroyed in the presence of truth? When truth is absent, there is a blind spot in our thinking that allows deception a dwelling place. Be prepared to make adjustments in the way you perceive situations around you, as truth will expose your natural way of thinking, which is rooted in selfishness. When truth comes where it is needed it will expose our wrong thinking. It may make you feel defensive. Use this reaction to your benefit and let it be an indicator of the areas where the Lord wants to reveal truth to you. This truth, if received, will bring death to the fallen nature, for truth and deception, like light and darkness, cannot occupy the same space. Notice I did not say *change*. We do not need change; we need death to our sinful nature. We need an exchange of our old nature for His awesome nature. When we say someone has changed, it is true in a sense. More accurately though, a part of their fallen nature has given way to the truth of God's Word, and therefore Jesus is allowed to freely flow in that area. We have exchanged our nature for His nature, which is a picture of how the covenant works.

Far too familiar is the experience of getting so far in the pursuit of destiny only to experience once again the frustration of having to start over. We see this happening when we witness or experience long-term relationships suddenly separate because of an offense, a hurt, or a misunderstanding. Many years of trust building and character testing are forfeited or lost only to have to start over again forming and building new relationships. It is likened to the scene in nursery school when just as the blocks are perfectly arranged, someone comes along and levels them to the floor. We have all experienced it and have either successfully or unsuccessfully dealt with rebuilding or giving up. Certainly there is validity in the argument that our heavenly Father, in His mercy, is sometimes the hand leveling the blocks. It is certainly His desire for us to try again. We also have to stop, take a serious look at our history, and determine what the Lord is asking us to do differently. To continue to build and arrange in the same way, somehow expecting it to work, is what psychologists refer to as insanity. If it did not work in the past, there is a very good chance it is not going to work in the future. In most instances we are simply going around the same mountain. There may be different faces and a different setting because it is a different season, but invariably we find ourselves in the same place at the end of the journey. We find the situation is hauntingly familiar.

I believe you are tired of going around the same mountain. I believe you are at a point of wanting all your moves to count. I believe you are ready to allow the Lord to make the necessary adjustments, insuring this pattern ends. I have a saying: "Otherwise, I could go fishing. I don't need the practice anymore." The truth is we do not have the time to continue going around the same mountain again and again. Our moves must count, or we will not fulfill the call of God on our lives. We will not fulfill our God-ordained destiny. We all want to stand before Him at the end of our journey and hear those words, "Well done, my good and faithful servant" (Matt. 25:21).

It is a desire within each of us to be like our heavenly Father. He has placed within us the drive to do something great, to make a difference. *Never feel it is wrong to have these desires.* I believe we have very little understanding of the power the Lord wishes to entrust to us. But we must allow Him to prepare us for this assignment if we are to be able to perform in His likeness. Rest in the Lord and trust Him to bring His will to pass for you in His ordained time. Always remember, He is the Developer and the Promoter. Yielding to the temptation of selfish ambition and self-promotion will send you on a long and arduous detour of frustration and delay.

Furthermore, it must be settled in your thinking that an adversary exists and is relentlessly placing stumbling blocks in your path to deter you from fulfilling your destiny. To deny the existence of this strategy is to foolishly set yourself up for ambush. As we proceed, it will be necessary for us to be in agreement on some fundamental beliefs; otherwise, you will be in disagreement with much of what is to follow.

Fundamentally, this book is based on the belief that, as a believer, there is a God-ordained destiny for your life. You have been called to greatness in the kingdom of God. Because of this, God's adversary, and therefore your adversary, will attempt to hinder and stop your advancement. In defiance of this resistance, you must walk in the authority Jesus was crucified to give you by walking in obedience to His words and commands. The way to victory has been provided through the shed blood of Jesus on the cross. The authority was given to us as believers to again take dominion over the things of this world. Being a follower of Jesus Christ assures reconciliation with your heavenly Father and eternal life in His presence. However, to fulfill your destiny on this earth, you must be an overcomer. You must walk in the authority Jesus provides. You must walk in obedience to His commands. And you will be resisted. Jesus never promised we would not be resisted. Jesus promised we would suffer persecution and tribulation (1 John 16:33), but He also showed us that we could overcome by the blood of the Lamb and the word of our testimony. And we are not to love our lives unto death (Rev. 12:11).

We must fight the good fight of faith; we must finish our course. We will never accomplish this without His grace abounding to us, which only comes through submission to His training in our lives and obedience to His directives. The call we each have requires being crucified with Christ; the reward is that we are able to reign with Him. We play a part in this. We can allow the Lord to train us, or we can refuse Him. It is possible to believe in Jesus but refuse His continued hand in our lives. If that is the case, you will not fulfill your destiny on this earth. If you believe that because of Jesus' victory on the cross, you are automatically untouchable to the devil, you are ignorant of your enemy's devices.

The truth is that Jesus has overcome your adversary, and you can share in that victory *if* you walk in obedience to Him. Teachings that deny the existence of an active enemy in your life are unscriptural. While obedience sounds like a simple and easy requirement, it will require you to operate in direct opposition to your natural born nature. However, when you yield to the lordship of Jesus, you will walk free in the liberty He died to give you.

It must further be settled that the power dwelling in us as believers is greater than any power dwelling in the world. Understanding this will prevent us from taking for granted what the Lord has provided, and it will prevent us from giving power to the enemy by fearing him. Let it rest in your heart at this moment that the enemy will only have the power you *knowingly* or *unknowingly* give him. He is a great deceiver, and if he can deceive you into believing something contrary to the Lord's Word or keep you ignorant of the Word, you will relinquish power to him in that area.

To fulfill our destiny, we must walk in submission to the Lord and in the authority we have been given by Him. But we cannot walk in something we do not know. We must know the one we serve, not just know *about* Him. For, to know Him is to love Him;

to love Him is to want to be with Him; and to be with Him is to know Him more. We often get this backwards. We try to know all about Him so we can walk in His power, and yet we do not really know Him. This leaves a wide gap for deception to find its way into our thinking. These areas of deception are where the enemy will gain access and pull us off course and into error.

While we need to acknowledge that an enemy exists and learn to recognize his devices, that is not to become our focus. When visiting the everglades, I need to know there are mosquitoes that are most prevalent at certain times of the day and that there is a specific repellant that is best to use. The mosquito is not to become my focus. It is a distracter that will harass me, try to take from me, and severely interfere with my journey. I do not visit the everglades to attack mosquitoes. I visit to explore the wonders of the everglades. The more I know about preparing for the unfortunate harassment of the mosquito, the more my mission will not be sidetracked and hindered by this unfortunate challenge. This is the way the Lord desires for us to know about and prepare for the devices used against us by the enemy. He desires to alter our vantage point so that we do not *look* for stumbling blocks but are prepared and challenged by their existence. They are certainly placed there by the enemy to take us out of the race. But, here is the good news: your Father uses them to qualify you as an overcomer. These strategies are part of our training, and proper response to trials brings promotion. When we encounter difficulty with keen discernment as to its origin and purpose, we will use it to our advantage and be challenged by its existence. We are to be as the eagle and allow the winds of adversity to take us higher.

Do track runners hate the hurdle? Of course not! Instead, the hurdle becomes a challenge to athletes as they determine how close they can come without knocking it over. This enables the runners to lose the least amount of time on the race and expend the least amount of energy on the jump. The Lord desires this for us in our spiritual race. He wants us to see the hurdles as an opportunity to demonstrate our confidence in Him, which is an indicator of our spiritual fitness level and development. In this way, we will overcome them, expending the least amount of time and energy possible.

As we learn to deal with the hurdles as they come and get over them quickly, it will be as if we hardly noticed the obstacle in our way! Remember that we are made in the likeness of our Father. He does great exploits, and I have come to believe that He absolutely beams when His children defeat and overcome the strategies laid against them.

I recall a conversation I had with the Lord one day as I was talking to Him and doing some complaining about all of those daily frustrations that come to test us. I said to Him, *Lord, I love You with all of my heart, and I will forever serve You in the face of adversity, but I sure will be glad when this gets easier and I no longer have to put up with this stupid kind of stuff.* I heard Him very clearly say to my spirit, "The resistance will never get better. As a matter of fact, it will intensify. What will change is you. You will get better at not allowing it to distract you; you will become more able to focus in the face of adversity; and you will get to the point that you hardly notice it at all."

That day I realized the enemy of my God and the enemy of my soul was on a mission and he was not going to ever give up on this earth. I realized what it meant to walk in the overcoming power of Jesus. I realized the only way to not notice was to allow the Lord to bring death to the soul-centered reactions that are only natural to the human being.

Returning to our athletes example, it is important to remember the runners only clear the hurdles in their lanes. You never see a runner jump lanes to clear all the hurdles on the track. Just imagine the disorder that would be brought to the race if the runners did not stay in their respective lanes. This is a wonderful picture to guide us.

We are exhorted to run *our* race. We will see many hurdles, but we are only called to clear the ones in our lane. The enemy loves to get us off course by bringing to our attention hurdles on the perimeter. Ignore them; they are not in your direct path. They are distractions designed to keep your eyes from where they need to be. They are designed to keep us running everyone else's race except our own. When you notice you are being drawn to give your attention to a perimeter situation, be alerted. There may be something in your direct path the enemy is trying to keep you from seeing. We each need to be faithful to get in our assigned place and to stay put!

With each stumbling block, our choice will be to obey or to go our own way. Obedience will bring overcoming power. As we submit to His lordship, He is able to operate through us at a higher level. When this happens, it is like a skater getting a new skateboard. Being accustomed to the old one, he may not operate the new one as easily. The footing is awkward. The skater who is aware he or she has a new board may be easier to understand than the example of a servant being promoted to a new assignment. As servants, we often do not understand what has taken place, and we actually think we have gone backwards. When the Lord orchestrates a trial for us to be tested and we respond to this test in obedience to His commandments, we can be encouraged that the Lord is ready to advance us to the next stage of learning and development. Therefore, we are in new territory and will feel awkward in the beginning. We will hear ourselves saying something like, "If I could only get back to the way I was..." Be encouraged; you will never be the way you once were. You have passed that place, never again to visit. Keep looking forward, keep trusting Him, and before you know it, you will be doing tricks on your new board. You will regain your footing. He is faithful!

I have often heard it said, "Higher levels, bigger devils." While this is certainly true, let me tell you what the Lord spoke to my heart.

Many of the attributes we see and admire in the soul of man are shadows of our awesome God. For instance, who cannot be touched by the heart of an athlete giving his all to perform, the eye of the tiger for conquest, and the precision of performance no matter what the activity? There is something intangible that strikes a chord in the spirit of man, moving us when we witness excellence. These are very natural abilities, and they fall very short of the ability of God. However, they are a shadow of what man was meant to be. They are sometimes a shadow of one small facet of God. I believe our God is a very competitive God. He is victory. He is excellence. He loves to demonstrate His power through His own people.

There is a management principle that must be applied in order for anyone to successfully perform a task to which they have been assigned. It is simply this: you must be given authority commensurate with your responsibility. Have you ever been asked to perform a function that you had not been given the authority to carry out? This is a very frustrating and difficult situation. The effective manager knows that authority is a key to successful performance. Many of the principles used in management are found to be scripturally sound. Our Lord Jesus, upon departing this earth, gave the commission to His church and immediately delegated the authority for the task. Be confident; you will always be given the authority to carry out your assignment. This means you will always be given the power to overcome that which stands in your way. Higher levels, bigger weapon! You can count on it! It is His way!

So, we are to focus on our powerful God. We are to be aware of the enemy but maintain our line of sight on the One who is the victor. Once we have received the Lord's instruction, focus is the essential element that must be maintained in order to overcome the stumbling block. This is because stumbling blocks are expressly designed to break our focus. As you allow the Lord to complete His work in you, you will begin to develop spiritual strength and discipline that will result in your being more in tune with your spirit man than your natural nature. This is the training that will allow you to ignore rejection, misunderstanding, mistreatment, and betrayal, while all the time maintaining focus on the Lord's mission in the heat of battle. Unbroken focus will never come with will power alone. Will power is of the soul; it is rooted in pride and is no match for the enemy. Just as the Lord is a spirit and you must worship Him in spirit, the enemy is also a spirit, and you must battle him in the spirit, in the power of the only One who defeated him. The Lord has given us His Spirit so that we may walk in victory, but there is much self-will that must be removed before we will choose to do things His way!

The strength to stand in the will of God will only come by the grace of God and must be developed with training that involves the death of our will and submission to the Lord's will. We will, in a very small way, become intimately aware of what our Lord was feeling when He said, "Not my will" (Luke 22:42, NIV). He does require us to share just a little piece of that suffering.

Here is another word picture to help you as you proceed through the chapters. I am originally from the state of Kentucky, and in the spring, the lakes do something we call "turning." Because the air temperature on top of the water is becoming warmer, it causes the cooler water in the bottom to rise to the top, forcing the water on top to become mixed with the bottom. The result is muddy water for a few weeks.

Now, take this picture and apply it to experiencing a change in season with the Lord. This is what you experience during times of transition or times of going from one season in God to another. At these times of transition, circumstances become unclear. And these are the times when you will be trained to trust God without training wheels. During these times, you may feel as though you don't fit. You may have thoughts that tell you you've lost your edge and that you are a fake and if anyone knew your struggles, they would be so disappointed in you. It is in this period where you are most vulnerable to being tripped up by the enemy.

These are the times when you must hang on to God with all you have. These are the times when you will either stand and see the salvation of the Lord or you will begin to function in your own strength and according to your own understanding. You will function from your soul or you will trust God. If you will stand—if you will trust Him in spite of all that is screaming to the contrary—you will overcome. You will overcome because of Him, not because of anything you will do in your own strength. You must come to that place where you say in your heart, *I have nowhere to go unless He sends me, nothing to say unless He prompts me, nothing to do unless He assigns me.* When you can come to this point of being willing to stand ready to do nothing unless He empowers you, you have come to the place where you are living for an audience of One, and God can do mighty things through you when He chooses.

Be encouraged that when things are unclear, you have been given the opportunity to trust Jesus out of obedience. Trusting Him out of obedience will put you in a position of great trust. No matter what it looks like—no matter what it feels like—you can always know He is there. He will never leave you, He will never forsake you, He will tell you what you need to know when you need to know it. (See Heb. 13:5.) As an act of your will, you must keep your focus on Him and what He has instructed you to do. If He is saying nothing, it is because He has already told you what you need to know. There comes a time when He does not repeat Himself every day. He expects you to trust Him.

I sincerely believe that if you will endure through the chapters of this book—if you will purpose not to survive them but to allow truth to bring death to your natural, soul-centered nature by the work I believe the Lord wants to do through them—you will emerge stronger and leaner and better fit to serve Him. If you are ready to proceed, let us begin to examine these stumbling blocks. It is my sincere prayer that you begin to take the liberating truths to follow and walk in a grace you have not known before. I pray you would walk in a level of victory that is more exhilarating than anything you have ever experienced. The great basketball coach, Adolph Rupp, was recited the famed Grantland Rice line, "When the one great scorer comes to write against your name, he marks not that you won or lost, but how you played the game." To this Coach Rupp replied, "Well now, I just don't know about that. If winning isn't so important, why do you keep score?"[1] I agree with Coach Rupp. Your heavenly Father has a pure winner's heart. It does matter whether you win or lose. Do not be discouraged if you lose a battle, but be determined you are going to win the war. Jesus has already won. The Father's heart is for you to be standing with Him, sharing in the victory you are destined to experience.

Certainly we do not want to go looking for trouble, but there is a strength the Lord wants to give us. It lets us see a hurdle on the horizon. It is in our direct path, and we can say in our hearts, *Come on devil, make my day!* We are so confident of victory, not because of our ability, but because we know Jesus is in our right flank. If you have a revelation of how He wants you to operate in His great strength and power, you too can be as the young shepherd boy who looked in the face of a giant and exclaimed from the abundance of his heart, "Who is this uncircumcised Philistine that he should defy the armies of the living God?" (1 Sam. 17:26, NIV).

Destiny calls. Let's go!

Carryover Thoughts

- You have a God-ordained destiny.
- Your adversary, the devil, has a plan to stop you.
- Jesus is the Overcomer, and through Him you can become an overcomer too.

- Stumbling blocks are a part of your training and can work to your advantage.
- Higher levels of responsibility bring higher levels of authority.
- Your main battle is for focus!

Chapter 2

THE STUMBLING BLOCK OF SELF-CORRECTION

Oh, foolish Galatians! What magician has cast an evil spell on you? For you used to see the meaning of Jesus Christ's death as clearly as though I had shown you a signboard with a picture of Christ dying on the cross. Let me ask you this one question: Did you receive the Holy Spirit by keeping the law? Of course not, for the Holy Spirit came upon you only after you believed the message you heard about Christ. Have you lost your senses? After starting your Christian lives in the Spirit, why are you now trying to become perfect by your own human effort?

—Galatians 3:1–3

I am not one of those who treats the grace of God as meaningless. For if we could be saved by keeping the law, then there was no need for Christ to die.

—Galatians 2:21

As we endeavor to walk in the destiny the Lord has for us, we will forever battle to maintain focus on Him. His Word tells us we are to be made into His image. This is a lifelong journey and one the enemy attempts to disrupt in the beginning of our walk with God. One of the most distracting strategies he uses is to divert our focus from our Lord and Savior, Jesus, to ourselves.

The enemy of our soul is relentlessly attempting to get us to focus on how we must change to bring us to where we are pleasing to the Lord. If we take this bait, we will begin to try and figure out what steps we must take to qualify for our Lord's favor. If we are not careful, we become totally self-focused and self-consumed, all the time thinking we are pleasing the Lord. It grieves His heart, and He must resist our prideful attempts to make ourselves good enough for Him.

So how are we to be made into His likeness? Our focus must be on *Him.* We are to sit in His presence, behold Him, be obedient to what He is asking of us, and by this, be made into the image we are beholding. If we are beholding Him, we will become like Him. If we are beholding our faults, we will continue to walk in those faults. I pray your mind be renewed so you may comprehend this truth. We *become* what we *behold.* (See 2 Cor. 3:18.)

Did your mother ever say: "I can tell you've been hanging around so-and-so, because you're acting just like them!"? Well, she was probably right. We just have a way of acting like those we keep company with. It is the same principle. If we hang around Jesus, we will begin to act like Him. We come into His presence to become like Him; we do not wait until we feel we are good enough. He does not sit and wait for us to walk by for inspection; He sits and waits for us to sit at His feet and fellowship with Him. When He is ready to make a change in us, He does it in a way that lets us know that without Him it would never have been possible. We give Him all the glory, because we really know it was all Him!

It must forever be settled in our minds that we cannot effectively change ourselves. Even if we know what needs to be changed, we could not make the change. When the Lord is working in us, He is making deep, deep adjustments we could not understand even if He were to explain them. He is making the adjustments as we behold Him. Our attempts to help Him will only hinder and delay the process. (See Phil. 1:6.)

Those areas we observe in our lives and in the lives of others that fall short of the Christ-likeness we desire are rarely the problem anyway. They are symptoms of the problem. For a woman to use cheek color does not solve an unhealthy blood condition making her face pale. Correcting behavior misses the target—the *real* problem. The Lord knows the real problem and, if allowed access to our lives, will make the necessary adjustments. The symptoms will go away in time. We must focus on Him, allowing Him to work, and when He wants us to do something, He will tell us. Our job is to quickly obey.

Acts of Obedience Are Your Only Requirement

When we allow ourselves to fall into the trap of self-correction, we become vulnerable to a doctrine of works that is promoted by a religious spirit. This is the enemy's attempt to take the place of the Holy Spirit. He attempts to tell you how to make yourself holy. Save yourself a lot of time and aggravation. You cannot ever, no matter what you do, make yourself holy. Only God is holy and by believing in His Son, trusting in Him, and being obedient to Him can you be holy.

You can also recognize the influence of the deception, because it will always try to get you to be concerned with your appearance. It influences you to be concerned with "ironing" your personality "wrinkles" before washing them. As believers we are clean by what Jesus did on the cross (1 Cor. 6:11). Once we are washed in this way, we need very little ironing. But if we continue to try to make ourselves acceptable, the enemy will see to it that we have just enough success to be deceived, and we will then fall into the trap of becoming proud of our accomplishments. At this point, we will become a victim of the worse deception of all—self-righteousness. Appearance will become more important than relationship. We will begin to live with a consciousness of what man thinks and will lose our sensitivity to what the Lord knows. It is a destructive cycle where deception becomes stronger and where we become more removed from the intimate relationship the Lord so desires for us to have with Him.

Remember, it is not less of you that will provide for more of Him. It is more of Him that pushes out the old you. When these two are backwards, you will lose the joy of your salvation. You will not lose your salvation, but you will lose the *joy* of your salvation. It will choke the life and the joy from your walk with the Lord. Condemnation will cloud your mind or pride will cause you to think of yourself as better than others. Either way, you are not walking in the righteousness Jesus died on the cross to give you. The Book of Galatians earnestly warns of another gospel. (See Galatians 1:6–7.) It is so subtle; it so easily seeps in to contaminate our thinking. Ask yourself, *what is my focus?* If it is to make yourself more acceptable to others, or to the Lord, you have fallen prey to this deception, this false gospel. Our desire for change should be for the sole purpose of pleasing the Lord just because we love Him. It should be because we want to please Him out of love for Him, not because we are trying to win His love or favor. You already have that.

The Lord is the One who made you, and He is the best candidate for the task of perfecting you. You will be perfected by just sitting at His feet in His presence, by reading His Word, by speaking with Him, and by becoming familiar with His voice. Messages, sermons, teachings, and books will also bring you into His likeness as long as they carry the heart of the Father by the authority of His Word.

When I was a new believer in Jesus, I was given a wonderful education by someone fresh out of Bible school. He just wanted to preach the gospel and tell people about the Jesus he loved. To sit under that type of teaching is the greatest gift a newborn believer can be given. The gospel was preached week after week; the good news was declared over and over. I began to notice my life was changing without realizing how or when. Patterns in my life began to disappear when I came to know this wonderful Friend named Jesus. Never once did I hear a sermon saying, "Don't do this" or "Don't do that." Jesus was set before me, and I beheld Him. I only heard the good news, and I began to do the things the Lord encourages us to do. Simply stated, they replaced other things without my noticing in the beginning. My language changed, what amused me changed, my attitudes changed, my desires changed, and those whose company I enjoyed changed. So many changes and not once did anyone have to tell me to stop anything.

Thank God for a gospel that will change a man instead of a gospel that tells a man he has to change! (This is not to imply the Lord will never send someone along to tell us to stop doing something. However, when this occurs, He has already been dealing with us in that certain area, and we know we have been skirting an issue that is of importance to the Lord.)

As I matured in the Lord, I began to be aware of my faults as the Lord brought them to my attention. However, I believe the key was that *He* brought them to my attention. I loved Him, and I wanted to make myself pleasing to Him as a bride would her groom. My motivation was love, not works. Anytime we believe we must make a change to be acceptable to God, aside from accepting Him as our savior, we have believed another gospel. It is not the gospel of Christ. This gospel clearly tells us that we are acceptable to Him *even though*, not *because*.

The natural, logical mind wants to reason some way to make us acceptable. It sounds good, but it doesn't work! Man can effect a change in his behavior for a season. He may be able to sustain the change for a long period of time, but eventually, if the inner man has not been transformed, the outward behavior will return. Only the Lord can change a heart. When the heart is changed, it is then possible for the outer man to manifest the inner work. To focus on yourself for the purpose of being acceptable to the Lord is a strategy of the enemy to have you become self-focused.

This is another word for self-centered, which is another word for selfish. These adjectives are a description of the carnal nature and a description of the enemy of our soul.

When our eyes are on the one who created us, we will frequently be aware of how far we are from being like Him and at the same time how much He loves us anyway. This constant reminder of His goodness is the fertilizer for humility in our heart and what allows Him to make the necessary adjustments in our nature. It is the goodness of the Lord that draws a man to repentance. Repentance is an act of humility. It is not the Lord's heart to work humility in us through humiliation; this is His last resort. It is His goodness that works humility. If we are hardheaded, he will allow us to experience humiliation because of His mercy. Let me say it again—it is His last resort. He loves us, therefore He is patient with us. He is so very long-suffering!

Our minds have a very difficult time processing this truth, because it is so contrary to our natural way of thinking. Usually what wants to surface is the thought, *If we are acceptable to the Lord just the way we are, then there is no reason to ever be any different.* We may conclude that His unconditional love means that we can rest in His approval without ever changing. Sorry, that won't work either. Be assured, we all need more changing than we can imagine. There is more wrong with us than we will ever comprehend. But, He has a plan to turn us every which way but loose. However, it is only the One who created us who can make the adjustments. He does love us just the way we are; He will never love us anymore or any less no matter what we do.

He has a plan for us, and as we are obedient to His instructions, the transformation of Christlikeness comes forth. When we approach the Lord in this manner, we are as clay in His hands. When we approach Him by trying to please Him and by being acceptable to Him by the fruits of our labor, we have approached Him in pride. He must, in obedience to His Word, resist us. Cain attempted to give to the Lord a portion of his labors, something he had produced, and his sacrifice was unacceptable to the Lord. Abel, on the other hand, gave to the Lord only that which the Lord had produced, and the offering was acceptable. The only sacrifice we can take to the Lord to find acceptance is the spotless Lamb that was slain. We go to the Father through Jesus. Any other way will bring His resistance and rejection.

It is the fallen nature of man at work when we try to accomplish right standing with the Lord through our own works. The root of this behavior is pride. God honors His Word, and He has established the principle of resisting the proud and giving grace to the humble. It does not matter how sincere we are; it is a law of the God of this universe to resist pride. To come to Him with works guarantees His resistance. To come to Him in humility guarantees His grace.

Grace

The grace of God is the only means by which we will act like God. There is no other way. As we behold Jesus, we come to know Him; as we come to know Him, we become confident in Him; as we become confident in Him, we become strong in humility; and as we become strong in humility, His grace can abound to us in ways we never imagined.

You will never conquer pride, selfishness, or any work of the flesh by striving on your own, but you can be encouraged that He has already conquered them. As you walk with Him daily, you will not fulfill the lusts of the flesh. Look away from yourself and behold Him, and you will find you are becoming more like Him. Do not allow outside influences to direct your attention to yourself. Look to Him and trust Him to transform you. This is a fundamental truth of God's Word—we become what we behold. To attempt change any other way will direct your focus onto yourself. This is self-correction; the root is pride, the fruit will always be strife and self-centeredness, and, at best, the results will be temporary. When the one who created you is ready to make an adjustment, He will give you an instruction, and with that instruction will be an abundant supply of His grace. Your part is to walk in obedience to the instruction you have been given.

It is difficult to know what the Lord is asking of us when many people in our lives try to transform us. It is often said, "If you don't want to be hurt, stay out of the church." Unfortunately, we have earned that reputation. People operating in underdeveloped gifts of ministry cause much of the damage. We think we are walking in truth and discernment when we are actually walking in pride and yielding ourselves to a critical and judgmental heart. We have all been on the receiving end of this, and most importantly, we need to admit that we have all been guilty of judging and criticizing others. The Lord has given us a wonderful antidote for this behavior; it is called *love*. Walk in it, forgive, ask the Lord to forgive you, and go on. You are going to be hurt and misunderstood; you must forgive and trust the Lord.

So how do we know what the Lord is focusing on in our lives? Again, if we are not careful, this question may cause us to fall into the trap of self-focus. I have found in my walk with the Lord that I am usually not aware of His workings until very near completion. Have you ever had the experience of suddenly realizing you were different but not being able to determine exactly when the change occurred? Certainly it was not immediate, but gradual enough not to be noticeable. I am convinced the Lord does this intentionally; otherwise we would attempt to help Him. Usually, toward the end of the adjustment, He will orchestrate a situation that presents the opportunity for us to walk in what we have learned. Then we realize a great work has been done in our hearts for which we can take no credit. That feeling, that realization of what He did through you and in spite of you, is the fruit of humility.

Circumstances do not make us what we are; they provide a platform to show us what we are. It is also important to guard against being influenced by what others are doing. The Lord may be dealing in one person's life concerning giving. He may be teaching them to be obedient to His voice when He asks them to give. However, He may be working in a person who is quick to give to teach them to listen to His voice about who to give to and when. Our focus must be Him, not what He is doing in the lives and ministries of others. I believe this tendency to focus on what others are doing and following in their steps is the reason for many falling short of the blessings of obedience. *Sacrifice is noble, but obedience produces blessing.*

When the Lord focuses on a specific area in your life, you will begin to hear it in everything around you. As you read His Word, there will be a common subject that continues to surface. As you listen to music, hear a sermon, or watch a TV program, you will continue to hear the same theme. The Lord has a wonderful way of illuminating those areas He is dealing with at the time. (See Prov. 1:20–21.) You will not be able to get away from the subject easily. If you resist the prompting, your heart will begin to harden and deception will find a place to dwell. Seek Him and trust Him. As you begin to yield to Him, you can trust Him to lead you into the knowledge of the truth.

Sometimes the subject will come to us through criticism and accusation. Although this is not the Lord speaking to us through evil words, He has given us a very simple principle to use, causing it to work for our good. Jesus instructs us to agree quickly with our adversary. (See Matt. 5:25.) This revelation accelerated the work of the Lord in my life in a very significant way. I will share something I learned through experience.

Under attack

When the accuser of the brethren begins to criticize you, rather than being defensive, quickly go to your Father and ask Him if there is any truth to what is being said. I have been amazed at how the enemy will try to send a fiery dart and how the Lord will allow the dart to expose a weakness in us, forever changing us for the better. The Lord will take what the enemy is attempting to use to harm us and actually use it for our good. I can only explain this by an example in my life.

A few years ago I went through an intense trial—one we must all eventually endure—when everything within me was challenged. Everything the Lord imparted to me was questioned and viciously attacked. Even though I knew it was not true, I felt forsaken by the Lord. When you go through this trial, the heat and pressure purges error and drives truth deep within your spirit. Truth becomes a part of your bones. During this time of testing, I experienced intense teasing concerning how much I talked. All my life I have had the reputation of being a talker; being teased was something I grew up experiencing. I always felt loved and appreciated for who I was. I never felt criticized and mocked. There is a teasing done in love that causes a person to rejoice in their uniqueness, and there is also teasing the Lord refers to as "corrupt communication" (Eph. 4:29, KJV). The latter stings the heart like a dart. My heart felt the darts, and I was not sure what the Lord was saying or whether He was saying anything.

This went on for quite some time. One Sunday, a visiting evangelist spoke in our church. This man did not know me. During his message, he spoke on how the Lord changes people. In the course of the sermon, he made the statement, "The Lord is trying to get some of you to talk more, and He is trying to get some of you to *shut up*!" When he spoke the last words, he walked right in front of me, leaned over, and spoke the words in my face, personally, directly, and firmly! Needless to say, I was the object of a great laugh. I laughed too, but I was not amused. My heart was crushed!

You may say this was simply coincidental, but I believed this man was being totally led by the Holy Spirit. I was hurt and confused.

Getting from the service to my car could not happen fast enough for me. I wanted some answers from my Father. Two seconds out of the driveway, I began to cry out to Him. I needed to know once and for all what He was trying to teach me. The Lord spoke so clearly. He is such a faithful God, and He will give us wisdom if we will simply ask. He told me He was not pleased with the coarse jesting. It was disrespectful, and the teasing was an attack from the enemy of my soul to discourage me and to shut me up. However, He went on to tell me that He too was trying to shut me up. Not from being the talker I am, but from speaking the information I was speaking.

There is information the Lord may share with us to give us understanding of a situation or insight into a problem. This information can provide direction for how we can pray, or it can be used as a platform from which we can speak truth. It is meant for us only and not for us to repeat. For instance, the Lord may grant you the insight that an acquaintance is deeply bitter from a betrayal. This information may help you better understand things they do or say that you may not otherwise understand. Rarely are we to share this information with anyone. We can simply be ready to speak *from* the information *as the Lord orchestrates the circumstances,* and we can also use the information to begin to specifically target our prayers for that person. The Lord will give us insight into a situation, because He wants to trust us to love a person and be faithful to pray for them. He doesn't give us information so we will look gifted to others. The gift is that we get to hear from God! The enemy did not want me to speak truth; the Lord did not want me to reveal knowledge. I revealed what the Lord allowed me to understand to gain the acceptance of man, and I withheld truth for fear of displeasing man.

The Lord very easily could have used this evangelist's gift of speaking the Lord's heart to say to me, "There are those who are teasing you, and I call it course jesting. They are being used of the enemy to shut you up from speaking truth." Certainly, this type of prophetic word is the dream of any student of the Lord whose flesh is crying out for vindication. Always know the Lord never pets our self-centered nature that desires to be affirmed no matter how much the enemy attacks. The Lord will actually allow the attack of the enemy to expose our selfish nature. There was a problem within me that the Lord had His finger on. There was something in me He was purging, and it was this problem that He was addressing. His affirmation of me later when He explained He was not speaking to me through the teasing was the oil being poured on my wound once He pulled out the tare. (See Matt. 13:30.)

You may ask, What was the tare? The tare was my inordinate need to be accepted and approved of by others. It was at the root of my behavior to talk about the things I believed the Lord may be showing me. My heart was motivated by wanting others to listen to me and by wanting them to know that I was hearing from God. Our lower nature loves for others to affirm and appreciate us. This is not such a terrible desire, but we must first and foremost have this from the Lord, and then it will be allowed to flow through others as the Lord deems appropriate. The Lord was actually dealing with two tares at the same time. The second was my fear of man that kept me from standing for truth. I had an inordinate need to be loved and accepted by others, and I withheld what I believed was the vantage point of the Lord at times for fear of being rejected. I wanted to be loved and appreciated and did not want to be at the center of anything other than complete harmony. My heart was motivated by wanting to please and be in the good graces of others. This is certainly not a bad desire, but when it exceeds our desire to please and be in the good graces of our Lord, it is a great problem. I was fearing man above God, and He was very pleased to reveal this to me.

Was the Lord the source of the information I had been allowed to gain for understanding purposes? Yes, I sincerely believe He was!

Was my heart sincere when I gave to others what He was giving to me? Mostly!

Was my motive pure as I moved in the gift the Lord had entrusted to me? Unfortunately, the answer was no, and it was His great pleasure to remove the tares.

I was grateful and I felt loved. The good news is He disciplines those who are His.

The Lord does not impart to us information in order to validate our gift. Actually our gift is not for us, but rather for those He connects to us. We can never wear our gift as a medal, but rather we are to yield that gift to the Lord as a piece of conduit through which He can flow on any given moment. We are not to have control of the "on" button, and we are not to have control of the "off" button. It is His life that is to flow through us as He wills!

I believe the evangelist was not aware of how he was being used to correct me. I sincerely believe he had no personal knowledge of me or my situation and that he was in no way being used to be hurtful or critical. How those words were heard and used by others in attendance was between them and the Lord. I chose to walk in obedience to God's instruction and to not be offended. I chose to allow the Lord to use the words for good. That adjustment immediately changed my walk with the Lord and increased what the Lord could entrust to me. Agreeing quickly with my adversary (who is the devil, not people) was one of the single most beneficial lessons I have ever learned. While the actions of the others were clearly not the Lord's heart, my being obedient to His command to not be offended allowed Him to use the trial to change me. I pray this incident will help you understand the importance of always seeking the Lord for His understanding and interpretation of the circumstances surrounding your life. It is an important step to becoming like Him and walking in His love. (See James 1:2–4.)

With His perspective comes His heart, and with His heart comes His words. With His words comes His power!

Our heavenly Father calls Himself our Father. This is the name Jesus used when referring to Him. We have to know and trust the Lord as the perfect parent. Within Him rests all the perfect attributes ideally contained within a natural father and mother. Think of the joy a child finds in living. Does a child strive to understand what he is to do next to be a better child? Not usually. A child is just that—a child. They go about their day trying to have fun and enjoy themselves. Parents are to establish guidelines and boundaries, and the child's responsibility is to obey. It is the wisdom of the parents that determine what the child needs.

Now, apply the same picture to our being raised in the Lord. It is the Lord who knows who we are and what we are being trained to do. He certainly uses more mature Christians to bring us along, and anyone entrusted with a little one of the Lord's must handle them as the Lord would. He will even use unsaved people to develop us. He is the one who orchestrates the circumstances. We will best walk in the joy of our salvation if we trust the Lord with a childlike faith. Be His child, rejoice in your liberty, and trust Him to develop you.

The enemy has enough dirt on us to keep us busy for a lifetime trying to earn our Father's approval. Be assured, as a believer you already have your Father's approval, not because of anything you have or have not done, but because of what Jesus did for you at Calvary. We all need an unbelievable amount of work done on us, but we cannot accomplish the work through self-correction and strife. It can only be accomplished by beholding the perfect One.

When you ask yourself who you are, the only accurate answer is, "I am in Him." Be at peace. Be still; all is well. He loves you, and when He is ready for you to do something, He will tell you. Acts of obedience are your only requirement.

Carryover Thoughts

- You cannot change yourself or anyone else!
- We become what we behold.
- You are in right standing with God, not because of you, but because of Jesus.
- Agree quickly with your adversary.
- Acts of obedience are your only requirement.

Chapter 3

THE STUMBLING BLOCK OF FORBIDDEN FRUIT

> People can tame all kinds of animals and birds and reptiles and fish, but no one can tame the tongue. It is an uncontrollable evil, full of deadly poison. Sometimes it praises our Lord and Father, and sometimes it breaks out into curses against those who have been made in the image of God. And so blessing and cursing come pouring out of the same mouth. Surely, my brothers and sisters, this is not right!
>
> —James 3:7–10

How many times have we judged Eve for eating from the forbidden tree and criticized Adam for his disobedience? We have heard the sermons preached from every angle concerning this fateful act by the first created humans. What I believe we do not always appreciate however is the state of innocence in which Adam and Eve existed. They had never seen or experienced death, they did not know or understand evil, and their entire existence consisted of dwelling in a paradise we can only imagine. Their habitation was a garden created by God, and their daily routine included communing with Him. Until they experienced the spiritual death caused by their disobedience, they had no precedent by which to comprehend the consequences of their actions. Certainly their innocence does not justify their error, but it does offer some appreciation for how devastated they must have been in their altered state. We, on the other hand, have witnessed the consequences of sin and we can learn from their experience. Let us look at the ways we too may be guilty of consuming this deadly fruit so we may begin to recognize the subtle ways it is put before us.

The Lord called the forbidden tree "the tree of the knowledge of good and evil" (Gen. 2:17). Adam was instructed to not eat of the fruit of the tree. It was placed in the garden to be seen, but it was not to be consumed. The Lord never instructed Adam not to look at the tree, only not to eat from the fruit. Why would the Lord allow us to see something and then limit our consumption? Certainly the Lord is not a tempter of evil, so what possible benefit is there in seeing if we are not permitted to partake?

One answer obviously is that obedience holds very little value if there is no opportunity to disobey. However, I want to explore another possible reason the Lord allows us to have knowledge and yet strictly controls what we are permitted to do with that knowledge.

Since the Lord allows us to be instruments of His restoration and reconciliation, this sometimes involves His entrusting us with knowledge. As He chooses, we are given insight or may be entrusted to discover sensitive information. In most instances when this occurs, we are to take the information and instead of repeating what we know (or think we know), we are to be obedient to the commandment to love and begin to believe for the best, hope for the best, and pray earnestly for the other. We are to begin to bless with our words and not come into agreement with the accuser of the brethren. We are allowed to see, and then we are allowed to speak the *truth*. Jesus is the truth, so if He wouldn't say it, it's not the truth! It may be *factual*, but it is not *truthful*. Facts change, but truth never changes! Here's the dividing line: we are allowed to see and judge what we see. In most instances, we are *not* allowed to speak what we see. This is the forbidden action. When we do this, we are consuming the fruit (taking it into ourselves) and offering it (telling it) to another. Another word for this is gossip. In doing so, we are partaking of death and offering death. When we see it, it is outside of us. When we speak it, it is being allowed to come into us and out our mouth. This is why Jesus said it is not what goes into a man that defiles him, but what comes out of him. It angers our Father's mind! It saddens our Father's heart!

We are allowed to see, and then, as we are obedient, the Lord gives us the authority to speak to a situation and dispel the darkness. Authority comes by walking in obedience to His ways. We are *not* allowed to see and speak the evil plan. This empowers the darkness. When it is dark, one cannot see! Deception is rooted in the plan of the enemy. We do not have the purity of heart to be judges. Mixture finds its way into our judgment, and we pass sentence on God's precious children. For this reason, He alone reserves the right to fully judge a situation; He alone reserves the right to execute vengeance and justice.

A good example of this, and one so many of us can identify with, is in raising our children. We may discover something about our child that is devastating to us, and we can all count on them to display behavior at times that is totally unacceptable. Let's say they are caught in a lie, refuse to do their chores, and treat us with disrespect. So, we are looking at the tree of knowledge, and the fruit we see is labeled, "lie," "disobedient," and, "disrespectful." We can take that information and do one of two things. We can judge it and yield to the accusations of the one who accuses us before God day and night, or we can look to the tree of life and pick the fruit of truth. Basically, we are allowed to choose who we are going to believe.

If we listen to the enemy, he will tell us our child is a liar and is lazy and that they do not love us. If we come into agreement with him and speak this out, we have taken one of the most powerful weapons the Lord has given us and used it to speak the words of the enemy to curse. While I'm sure four-letter words are not pleasing to the ears of the Lord, they don't hurt Him like speaking a word of judgment over His child. That is cursing.

If we choose the other route, we will cast down the thoughts of judgment, look to the tree of life, and begin to speak the truth of God's Word. He will tell us the truth. The truth is they are fearfully and wonderfully made. If they are faithful to repent, He is faithful to forgive. (See. 1 John 1:9.) He has a plan that is good and full of hope for them. As we begin to speak His heart that He reveals in His Word, we are blessing them with our words and repeating the plans the Lord has for them. We are using our words to shoot bullets for good, and they will shoot holes in the enemy's plan.

God will have you to judge and address the behavior and bring correction. The enemy has you judge the person and condemn the person. Herein lies the difference. Always remember to separate the person from the behavior. The person is made by God in His image. The behavior, if it is bad, is from the seed of Adam, and God has a plan to bring correction in that area.

Your enemy does not want you to get a hold of this powerful principle. Study this until the Lord gives you the revelation of how much power He has entrusted to you in your words. God is always waiting and willing to use a vessel for good. The enemy is always waiting and willing to use a vessel for bad. The power of life and death are in your tongue!

The Lord allows us to be ministers of His love, which, if received, will always bring restoration to a situation. He allows us to see from the tree of knowledge so we may immediately go to the tree of life, pick the fruit, and share it. He sets before us life and death and tells us to choose life.

Here is the internal struggle we all face:

Everything within the natural nature of man understands and wants to choose death. Most of the time, our enemy can sleep through these trials, because we are born with his basic nature. If we yield to that nature, we will be a vessel for him without him having to do anything! When we choose death, we are partaking of the tree of the knowledge of good and evil.

Everything within the nature of Jesus understands and wants to choose life. When we are His and His nature is inside us, He will give us the grace to override our natural tendencies and choose life if we obey. When we do that, we are partaking of the tree of life and His eternal life!

Genesis tells us that Eve ate the fruit because she saw that it was good for eating and knew that it would make her wise. She was curious and naïve—that is a dangerous combination! She ate and Adam ate, and spiritual death was the result. It was a guaranteed result in the garden, and it is a guaranteed result today. The tree of knowledge gives us information, but the tree of life provides the proper interpretation of the information. It is the tree we are allowed to partake of as a part of our inheritance. It is the tree that will always minister hope, understanding, encouragement, truth, and life. It will always give direction for properly handling what it is we know. When we partake of the knowledge of the forbidden tree and begin to speak that knowledge as if it were the truth, we have done what only the Lord is allowed to do. We have judged.

So, we must accurately interpret incoming information. With knowledge always come opposing interpretations, which compete for our attention. One is from the accuser; one is from the Lord. Let me offer a hint: The accuser badgers with accusations of judgment that play on our fears. The Lord speaks in a still, calm voice that renders peace and hope. One will be the vantage point of the Lord, and one will be a judgmental opinion perpetrated by the accuser of the brethren. We must learn to recognize our Father's voice.

To recognize His voice, it is necessary that we know not only His mind, but also His heart. His mind will always align with His Word and tell us what He *thinks* about a situation. His heart too will align with His Word and tell us how He *feels* about the situation and those involved. God hates sin, but He loves the sinner. If we know His mind but do not represent His heart, we may attach our emotional response to His mind. This is a very ugly thing to watch. It is what results in people blowing up abortion clinics. When our carnal heart mixes with God's pure mind, we risk taking matters into our own hands and may attempt to enact judgment. This is certainly not God's way. This combination does not have the proper balance of truth and mercy.

If we know His heart but not His mind, we may extend mercy that is unsanctified. This may result in our representing Him in a way that compromises the truth of Scripture. When we do this, we will embrace people in their sin. While we are to love them, respect them, and continue to pray for them, we must never alter the truth of Scripture to avoid their being displeased with us. When we do this, we are actually more concerned for what they will think of us then we are for their ultimate good by knowing the truth. Our actions indicate that we love ourselves more than we love them. True love stands faithful and committed to someone in the face of differences and regardless of the cost. It does not compromise truth to avoid conflict.

> But the wisdom that comes from heaven is first of all pure. It is also peace loving, gentle at all times, and willing to yield to others. It is full of mercy and good deeds. It shows no partiality and is always sincere.
>
> —James 3:17

I think it worth interjecting here the context of the above scripture. We are to be gentle, peaceful, loving, and kind, but we are also to love truth and not compromise its purity. We may hear the above words and think all communication is to be sweet, soft, pampering, and nonconfrontational. Keep in mind this verse was written by James, who wrote one of the most hard-hitting and confrontational books in the New Testament. It is the right combination of God's heart and His mind that will communicate truth in the perfect balance. Persons not wanting to know the truth will never hear it as peace loving. They want you to deliver a hybrid of the truth that affirms them in what they want to believe. This is not "first pure," and therefore not from the Lord's heart and mind. The truth is oftentimes not gentle, but the delivery of that truth must be. Is this not how the Lord deals with us? While we may not want to hear what He has to say, He changes not. His unyielding commitment to His truth is mixed with an equal part of His unyielding commitment to love us even in our sin.

We must represent Him with the perfect balance of His mind and His heart. We can only do this by operating in desperate dependence on Him. When we know Him and His Word, we can more accurately interpret those things we see and hear.

As we discussed in our example earlier, there is information that is factual and there is information that is truthful. Information is truthful if the heart of the Father is understood to interpret the situation in agreement with Him. Sometimes the facts of a situation are accurate but the conclusion drawn, based on those facts, is contrary to the truth. At this point, we have the mind of the enemy. If we listen and come into agreement with the accuser, we have attempted to do the job only the Lord has the right to do. We have judged. Sadly, more often then we realize, neither the facts nor the truth are present. Facts are just that—factual bits of information upon which conclusions can be drawn. Truth is what the Word of God says. Truth is eternal; truth never changes.

It may be a fact that a person is in complete disobedience to the commands of the Lord. Based on outward appearance, it may be totally impossible to believe they will ever amount to anything. But God's Word clearly states that we are His creation and that He has a beautiful plan for each of our lives. If we will repent and come to Him, He will restore and give us beauty for our ashes. (See

Isa. 61:3.) He doesn't qualify this promise by saying we must do this by a certain age. To allow ourselves to label a person hopeless, to allow ourselves to say they will never change, to allow ourselves to give up on them, is passing sentence on them. It is judging them. It is not the truth, no matter what the circumstances look like. At the very least, we should shut up and give no opinion. At the very best, we can begin to speak words of hope and truth over their lives based on God's Word.

The power of life and death is in the tongue. If we decide to operate in that power, it should be for good, not evil. I believe the ability to keep the mouth shut is the most difficult discipline to develop as a servant of the Lord. The single most significant indicator of spiritual maturity is not being able to quote Scripture or log in hours in prayer. I believe it is being able to keep your mouth shut!

Let us examine some of the ways information is packaged and how we are deceived into eating from the forbidden tree, allowing ourselves to be used by the accuser of the brethren.

Remember that the tree was in the midst of the garden in plain view to be seen. The question arises, How can we look upon something without partaking of the fruit? It is easy to understand with the tangible example of a tree, but with knowledge, it is difficult to distinguish between seeing and consuming. To see and not consume, you must do two very specific things. One, trust the Lord for all the knowledge He would chose for you to see and understand. Two, filter everything using the guidelines the Lord gives us for walking in love. If you are walking in love, you are walking in Him, and in Him is His heart.

Seeing through the law of love is being obedient to the one commandment Jesus gave us: to love one another as He loved us. (See John 15:12.) He laid His life down for us. He believed in us when we rejected Him. He did not give up on us when we were in rebellion. He believes the best, hopes the best, and rejoices not in our iniquity. He is never surprised by our shortcomings. Although He may be disappointed in our behavior at times, He never gives up on us. He is long-suffering. To say you owe no man anything but the love of God is to say you owe him a great debt. The love of God is the love with which the Father loved us, whereby He gave His only Son as a ransom for our debt. The love of God is the love with which Jesus loved us, whereby He laid down His life for us.

To trust the Lord for the knowledge He desires to come your way will require you to *deny your fleshly desire to "know things."* We are such curious beings, always wanting to have the whole story. It is better not to know anything until the Lord chooses to reveal information to us in His timing. This is how we most often eat of the tree of knowledge—by trying to gather information out of God's timing. There are things He desires us to know and with His wisdom allows us to understand. He knows our weaknesses and our frailties. He will protect us from information we are not prepared to handle, unless we are deliberately snooping around for it. When the Lord gives you information, His heart is also available for your understanding. You may or may not choose to approach it with His heart. This is your choice, but you have the means to make the proper choice in the beginning.

There are four primary weaknesses that will consistently cause us to choose to consume a forbidden fruit and not address it with the heart of the Father. They are selfish ambition, fear, envy, and pride. These enemies of our soul rear their ugly heads at every crossroads in our walk with the Lord. The enemy puts them there to trip us up. God allows them to be there to qualify us for promotion. Our heart response will determine the outcome.

Self-serving ambition will cause us to seek information for advancement and position purposes. Our concern will be for us and not for others. We will then begin to use the information to position ourselves and to compete with others for our supposed rightful place. It is the open door to betrayal! We will find that our competitiveness causes us to work situations for our advantage. To operate in this is to operate in disobedience, and this, according to the Bible, is another name for *witchcraft*. (See 1 Sam. 15:23.) Flee selfish ambition. Flee the temptation to operate in your own understanding and not in obedience to God's ways. They are guaranteed disqualifiers. Anything gained through this method will be a struggle and a curse in your life and will be a detour from your final destination.

The heart response of King David is such a good model for the way we want to respond. Even though Samuel anointed David as king, he refused to strive for the position. He returned to shepherding his sheep and waited for God's timing. There was much the Lord had to teach him with regard to shepherding if he was going to be entrusted to shepherd God's people. When he did become king and his throne was threatened, his consistent response to trust the Lord once again surfaced. His position was, "I did not put myself here, and I am not going to keep myself here. God put me here, and if He chooses, He can remove me" (2 Sam. 15:25–26, author's paraphrase). David was a fighter and a great warrior. He knew when to fight, and he knew how to win. But he was also a humble man, and he knew when not to fight. You never have to fight for where God has placed you. It is His battle.

Fear will cause you to seek information or make decisions for self-protection. Suspicion and doubt will cover the mind and thoughts like a cloud. You will find yourself mistrusting those around you and attempting to protect yourself from them. You will view and interpret them through a filter of suspicion, causing much misunderstanding. When fear is present, it births control. Liberty is absent. You cannot flow in an uninhibited manner. You will always fear you will make a mistake and you will not trust God to protect you. This is how the enemy severs God-ordained relationships.

The Lord does not connect us with another because they are perfect, and the fact that they are not perfect is not evidence that we are not to be connected. A suspicious mind is an open invitation for the enemy to plant all kinds of information for the purpose of division. Threats and intimidation will be a very effective tool of the enemy when fear is in operation. This information, often misinterpreted as discernment, is poison placed on our souls by the accuser of the brethren.

Again, the life of David is the story full of examples to understand this principle. The prophet Samuel, in obedience to the Lord's instruction, anointed David the king of Israel. While David knew what the prophet had spoken over him, he waited on the Lord's timing for this to come to pass. There is no indication in Scripture that David ever doubted God's ability to bring things about in His perfect timing. He simply served the Lord daily with a heart at rest because of his trust in his God. David's heart was fixed in the cement of trust. Even when he had what seemed to be a very justifiable reason to end the life of Saul, he refused. He stayed faithful, fully trusting God to be his defense. Every action on his part displayed his heart that sang, "He alone is my rock and my salvation" (Ps. 62:6). This is a beautiful psalm every servant of God will have the opportunity to sing. Sing it with all your heart. Sing it with tears running down your face, but sing it! If you find yourself in this place, it is an honor. It is your opportunity to lay down a very large hunk of your flesh, and when you do, you will be able to serve God at a level few walk.

This was the psalm that must have been ringing in David's heart as his son was threatening to overthrow his reign. Absalom's actions accused David of not being worthy to remain king. Once again, David had a choice. While his first choice dealt with the king in authority over him, this choice was about someone who was under his authority. David had every reason in the natural to squelch this uprising. He knew the Lord placed him in his position. He knew he was the one responsible for the Lord's people and their welfare. Was this not a different scenario? Would it not be appropriate in this situation to remove Absalom's threat to upset the kingdom? David's heart must have been very heavy. He was at risk along with all those over whom he was responsible. It is no wonder the Lord said he was a man after His own heart. (See 1 Sam. 13:14.) Once again, consistent with every trial he ever endured, David turned and left the matter to the Lord. He allowed the Lord to fight this battle. History gives us the outcome.

Envy causes us to seek information for the purpose of keeping score. It is the prevailing reason for dissatisfaction in our lives. We need to understand that the Lord is a good Father. He is well aware of our needs and wants. He is also well aware of what we are prepared to handle. If we do not have something we want, we must trust in His perfect timing. Envy will prevent us from being able to rejoice with others in their time of blessing.

Pride causes us to seek information, because we presume we are called to correct something. We think we have the answer, and if we can find out the details, we can correct the situation. Rest now in the knowledge that we cannot correct anything. The Lord is the Corrector. He may choose to use us as vessels; however, if this is the case, we will not have to go snooping for the information. It will find us. The Lord is the great Guide, and if we will trust Him, our steps will be ordered. If we will trust Him, our ears will be protected.

These enemies of our soul have one very destructive trait in common. They cause us to be self-focused. This will always result in tremendous torment. Rest in who you are and what you know. Rest in the timing of the Lord, and when information comes your way that stirs your soul to feel ambition, fear, envy, or pride, flee the temptation. If you can trust the Lord for the information He wants you to have, in the timing He wants you to have it, and handle it with a heart of love, you will not eat of the forbidden fruit.

Not only will you abstain from eating the forbidden fruit, you will also be a candidate for the Lord to use you for His purposes of healing and restoration. This means He may trust you with information that reveals weaknesses and error. When we have been entrusted with information having the potential to harm someone, we must be loyal first and foremost to the Lord. Remember that the Lord is always loyal to the truth. He is also loyal to us. Whenever you feel your loyalty to one person requires you to be disloyal to another, there is a very good possibility the information is not to be repeated. This information should never be divulged unless there is potential danger to others. This has to be a matter of great prayer. See yourself as a piece of conduit, and ask yourself, *What am I allowing to pass through my vessel?* You have been entrusted with this information for the purpose of the ministry of restoration and reconciliation.

Most of what we are allowed to know is not for the purpose of repeating. The fruit of the tree of the knowledge of good and evil includes the knowledge of offenses, weaknesses, compromise, judgment, criticism, gossip, faultfinding, discord, division, suspicion, unfaithfulness, fear, hatred, failings, faults, betrayal, bad memories, lost relationships, mistakes, errors in judgment, character flaws, and the list can go on and on. This would include anything resulting from the fallen nature of man.

Are these things accurate? Sometimes yes, sometimes no, and sometimes halfway. But they are not the truth.

The Lord commands that we love one another. What this involves is clearly defined in 1 Corinthians 13. When we look upon the tree of knowledge rather than partake of the fruit, it is our responsibility to stand in agreement with the truth of God's plan for the person or situation. At the same time, we must stand against what we see, refusing to come into agreement with the plan of the enemy. When we learn damaging information, it is usually the accuser of the brethren. We are being allowed to see the evil plan of the enemy. The Lord has a good plan for everyone; the enemy of God has a counter plan. There is much factual knowledge he can present to cause the people of the church to judge one another. Do not partake. It saddens the Father's heart!

Love does not deny that faults exist or that mistakes are not made. Love rather believes that no matter what exists or what has been done, there is hope for restoration and reconciliation. Love never writes off a person or a situation. Love believes the best, hopes for the best, trusts in the best, and covers. There is a just Judge. His name is God, and He is the only one with the right to pound the gavel and sentence a person. Love does not tolerate inappropriate behavior. It deals with it from a heart of helping the person overcome and leaving the matter to God to handle. If we get out of the way, God will handle it!

The single most important decision you will make concerning the human frailties of others is to *pray* rather than *discuss*. When you pray, you are seeing the fruit and returning it to the Father for handling. No matter how horrible a matter is, you can rest assured the heavenly Father loves that person with a love you will never fully comprehend. It is His desire to bring correction, healing, restoration, and reconciliation. The choice is set before us. We have an opportunity to pray or to judge. We can either come into agreement with the enemy, or we can come into agreement with the God who created us. Jesus is giving us an invitation to become His prayer partner. Agreement with Him carries power beyond our comprehension. This is one situation where so much can be won or lost by what we say.

To respond in covenant love does not mean we ignore error or wrongdoing. It does not require us to come into agreement with someone whom we feel is in error. It rather requires us to refuse to come into agreement with the enemy and believe that the person cannot and will not overcome. It requires us to be faithful to pray and to leave the matter to the Lord. I wish all would overcome;

unfortunately, it does not always work that way. However, it is not our place to give up on a person. Neither is it our place to take matters into our own hands and enact justice. The Lord may or may not choose to have you actively involved in their life, but you should always have a check on your heart making certain your thoughts and words toward them are good and full of hope and mercy so that you are forever willing to believe in them and for their total restoration.

It is critically important that we understand the seriousness of what is being taught here. The words of those who have God-given gifts and callings in the area of speaking carry much power. The degree to which you can help someone is the degree to which you can also hurt someone. The degree to which you have been called of God to speak is the degree to which you can be used of the enemy to speak. When you yield your gift to the evil plan of the enemy over a person, you have just spoken power to the evil plan. Therefore, the degree to which the Lord has gifted you is the degree to which power has been given to the enemy. Paul tells us in Romans 11:29 that "God's gifts and His call can never be withdrawn." When you have been entrusted with a gift from God you will have that gift even if you choose not to use it for God's purposes. And, if you choose to use it for your own purposes it will carry the influence you have been given. There are many musicians whose gifts are in operation and are advancing many things the Bible tells us to turn away from. But the gift these people have is undeniable and enduring. So, if you are using your gift for evil, it will still carry power. It will not carry what is referred to as *anointing*, which is God's life-giving power, but it will still carry power. Many do not discern the difference between God's anointing and the power of the enemy. With anointing there is power with the heart of God at the core. It ministers love, truth, correction, and hope. Its fruit is peace.

The words we speak carry power. They empower the unseen realm. Words of truth empower angels; evil words empower the enemy who only has the power we give him. He cannot speak his will over another. He must find a willing vessel that will do his talking for him. If we yield ourselves to speaking his words over another, even when it is factual information, we have allowed the enemy to use our words for harm. This is a very sobering thought, and I am sure there are instances coming to your remembrance that may cause you to shudder. But, our response should not be to fall into condemnation. The Lord loves you; His desire is for His children to understand this spiritual law and walk in obedience to His Word. In doing so, we will not only walk in safety but we can walk in His power and authority to bring healing and restoration to others by the words we speak.

Repentance is a wonderful gift. The Lord does not bring us to this understanding to condemn us, but rather to reveal a hindrance we may not be aware exists. Be obedient to not judge anyone, including yourself! Let us repent and move on.

You can actually take this stumbling block and turn it for good very quickly. As we have been discussing, the enemy has a counter plan for every person, while the Lord has a good plan for our lives. We know the enemy cannot create anything. He can only take that which is intended to be used for God's purposes and have us use it for evil. I have observed that the very weakness in a person is a counterpart to a strength the Lord desires to develop in them. For instance, show me a person with what the world calls *codependent tendencies*, and I will show you a person called to operate in a pastoral gifting. Show me a person who is stubborn and strong-willed, and I will show you a person who is called to walk in a place of unyielding commitment to truth. Is the codependency and stubborn behavior good? Of course not. But they are indicators of how a person has been constructed and how the enemy desires to use their traits for evil.

This is where we can speak faith-filled words over one another (Rom. 4:17). Remember that there is great power in agreement, whether we are agreeing with the Lord or with the enemy. Do not come into agreement with the enemy in your thoughts or in your words.

Just as we can cause harm with the words of our mouth, we have also been given the power to bless with our words. Speak well of one another. The day the church begins to cover one another with hope and love, not being quick to believe every accusation we hear, is the day we will begin to walk in an awesome power before the world. The Lord has told us that the world will know us by the love we have for one another. (See John 13:35.) This is not the kind of relationship where we buddy about, always smiling and never disagreeing. True love, the God kind of commitment we are to have toward our brothers and sisters, stands in the face of difficulty. It does not depend on feelings for guidance in building relationships.

We must also check our thoughts toward a person or a situation. Even when we have been obedient not to speak about what we know, information may alter our opinion or understanding. We must guard our hearts so that we do not judge. The enemy works very hard to sow discord among the brethren. When you gain knowledge, take it to the Lord as if it were a hot potato. He may very well be warning you of an area where you need to be careful. The enemy is trying to get you to judge, and the Lord is trying to protect you. As you seek Him on the proper interpretation, He will give you His heart, and you will be able to properly interpret and handle what it is you know.

There is absolutely no perfect person in this world. No matter how wonderful they may seem, they may falter and let you down. We all fall into this category. However, we are called to be connected to specific people, not because they are perfect, not because they are not, but because it is the Father's plan. We do not always have the choice of who we are to be connected with for destiny purposes. The enemy will work overtime and through any willing vessel to stop the joining together of those the Lord has destined to be joined together. When you allow this breech to occur, you have altered your destiny. It is knowledge from the tree of the knowledge of good and evil where information is revealed for the purpose of causing division.

There is a huge difference between acquiring spiritual knowledge and acquiring godly discernment. We are instructed to rightly discern. To rightly discern involves more than hearing or seeing information. It is to know information and have proper understanding. To know and apply your own understanding will lead you into error. You must have knowledge with godly understanding. Then you have properly discerned. When you take what you believe you know to the Lord, the vantage point He will give you on a situation is amazing.

Everything we have discussed to this point has concerned information that could be considered accurate but is in direct opposition to the truth of God. However, there is also information that is simply not factual. The enemy will go to whatever lengths necessary to bring division between people and therefore derail a mission. He will tell an absolute lie if there is a person willing to be a bearer of the lie or gossip. If he cannot find a person willing to lie or spread gossip, he will speak the lie directly to your mind. It is so necessary that you have the mind of Christ or you will be separated from the very ones you need and who need you. Again, to walk in covenant love with others will protect you and your ordained relationships.

We will never stop the enemy from attempting to bring division and therefore derailing a mission by separating us from others, but we can always refuse to listen to the accusations he wages against others, thereby thwarting his evil plan. The problem is not that he is a liar. The problem is we listen to him!

Carryover Thoughts

- It is still possible to partake of the tree of the knowledge of good and evil.
- Information we receive can be factual and not be the truth. This is forbidden fruit.
- How we handle what we know determines who we are serving.
- The power of life and death is in our tongue.
- Love does not deny a wrong has been done; it refuses to believe it cannot be overcome.
- Love never fails.
- Discernment is not only seeing, but understanding.

Chapter 4

THE STUMBLING BLOCK OF OFFENSE

> Those who love your law have great peace and do not stumble.
>
> —Psalm 119:165

The opportunity to be offended comes often and without notice. If you allow, it will stop your advancement and take you off course. Oftentimes it is without intent; sometimes it is with intent. Either way, it must be recognized and overcome. It is a basic rule of God's kingdom: we are to walk in covenant love with our brothers and sisters. Covenant love hears the voice of the Good Shepherd and refuses to listen to the tattling of the enemy. We are told to be kind, forbearing, and loving, esteeming one another in meekness. This chapter, however, is not intended to address the everyday call to operating in love and in freedom from offense. Rather, we will be focusing on times of promotion. It is in these times that one can have passed many tests of love by rising above the offense easily brought on by everyday interactions with people, only to fail the final exam. Listen very closely: at the end of every season in God, you must have the perspective of the Lord to advance to the next level. Your enemy will attempt to hinder this by giving you the opportunity to be offended. If you succumb, you will not have the Lord's perspective. Without His perspective, you cannot overcome and advance to the next level. At best, your movement will be lateral.

Offense comes to stir up strife, cause dissension among people, divide us from one another, and knock us off course. It is important to understand that although the Lord hates strife and does not tempt any man, He does allow offense to come, especially in times of transition when we are advancing from one level to the next. Your response will determine your promotion. The primary objective of this attack is to cause you to misunderstand the situation and therefore misunderstand the events to come. This is a good example of what we discussed in the previous chapter on the tree of knowledge and the tree of life. The tree of knowledge will often provide extremely accurate information—disclosing weaknesses, faults, and error—for the sole purpose of having you misinterpret what the Lord is doing. If this strategy is successful, you will not gain understanding. You will not have the mind of Christ and the wisdom of God. When your attention is drawn to facts that contradict the truth, your focus has been broken, and you will lose the vantage point of God every time.

Broken focus, no promotion

To prevent this, you must turn your face to the Lord and cling to His hem with desperate dependence. He will whisper in your ear what you need to know for understanding, and when you hear His whisper, you will shout with a shout of deliverance. This is actually a case where the saying, "Don't confuse me with facts. My mind is made up," will work to your benefit. When your mind is set on what God has said, the enemy will attempt to bring doubt by using facts. You must cast down everything that contradicts what God has told you, or else you will become double minded and will receive nothing from Him. There may never be another person to share in your understanding. Understanding this will advance you in levels of God unlike anything else I know. I pray you have ears to hear.

In speaking of the Lord's voice, I deliberately used the word *whisper*, because the Lord is not going to compete with offense to keep you from making a mistake. This is because you already have the knowledge of the truth needed to effectively handle the situation in obedience to Him. He tells you to choose life; He is not going to choose it for you. I will repeat. At the close of every season in God, you will be presented with a final exam that you must pass. Part of that exam will be the requirement that you perceive what the Lord is doing and not what the enemy is doing. The enemy behind the offense will bring to your attention things we are instructed by the Word of God to cast down. He is relentless, forever competing for our focus. The moment you give attention to the voice of the enemy, you have given him permission to place a blinder over your eyes and covers over your ears. You cannot listen to God and the enemy at the same time. If you will resist the devil and draw close to God, the devil will flee from you. The truth is he can't stand to be in the presence of the Jesus we serve. It is the presence of Jesus that causes him to flee.

Consistently, I have noticed a pattern in the Lord's dealings with me in this area. He will grant me His perspective. He will speak it very quietly to my spirit, where it is to become a standard by which all other incoming information can be compared. If I hold fast to what He has shown me and refuse to receive anything contrary to my first understanding, I will not be deceived. However, if I first hear the Lord and then entertain knowledge that is in direct opposition to what He has originally spoken to my heart, I have then given the enemy permission to bring deception to my mind. Once this deception is over our minds, it is very difficult to hear the voice of God in the situation. Confusion is a fruit of this snare, and confusion is always a huge red flag that the enemy is in operation! At this point, there is an urgent need for the intervention of the truth. My experience and observation has been that our lower natural nature resists with such stubbornness that out of pride we are tempted to justify our actions and even use Scripture as our defense. The only way out at this point is repentance. The longer you wait, the more deceived you will be and the harder your heart will be toward the voice of the Lord.

Have you been in a situation where you could see someone clearly being deceived and could not understand how they came to think or do what they were doing? Have you been on the other side of a situation and felt unable to understand how you had been so blind to your own error? We have allowed the enemy to blind us. By partaking of information contrary to what the Lord has previously spoken, we have opened a door to the enemy. This is a perfect opportunity to apply a principle taught of our Father. He promised us He will not allow temptation to come our way that we cannot resist. He will first give you His heart. Once you know His heart, the enemy will try to draw you away. If you bite, it is because you have knowingly refused to agree with what the Lord has spoken.

An offense may come by a person we are in relationship with, and it may not be a misunderstanding, but an actual betrayal. If the Lord has spoken that we are to be in relationship with the person, the act of betrayal does not automatically alter what the Lord has spoken. I am belaboring this point, because I believe it to be the key to walking in covenant love. When you walk in covenant love, you have tapped into a power unlike anything else. Our Lord is a very powerful God. He is love. Love is the power He works by. Faith works by love. These are statements we have heard and probably all said, yet do we really understand them? If we did, I believe we would operate in a greater dimension of His power. *Making* a mistake will not necessarily void a relationship; it is *refusing to correct* the mistake that may result in separation. Again, this is to be a decision made by the Lord. He asks us to forbear one another.

Allow Him to draw the lines. Separation may be necessary for a season, but always be open in your heart for reconciliation and restoration and moving on in the plan the Lord has for you.

Chapter 2 of 2 Kings illustrates the principle of this chapter. As we study the story of Elijah and Elisha, there are so many lessons to be learned. For the purpose of this chapter, I will discuss what allowed Elisha to receive the double portion of Elijah's anointing. Was it burning his plow and following the man of God? Was it his commitment to his mentor? Was it his relentless pursuit to continue on with Elijah? Was it his asking for the double portion that allowed him to receive from Elijah? No doubt all of these things were necessary, but did they provide for Elisha what was in his heart to have? I believe they were certainly prerequisites to being in proper position, but I do not believe they insured the impartation.

As Elisha traveled with his mentor, he was repeatedly told to stay back. Each time he refused, vowing to never leave his mentor's side. Following this relentless pursuit, Elijah finally asks of Elisha, "What can I do for you before I am taken away?" (2 Kings 2:9). Elisha was not shy, but plainly told Elijah he wanted a double portion of the anointing on his life. At that point, Elijah, realizing this was not within his power to give, but also knowing God's ways, instructed Elisha as to how he would be able to obtain the double portion he desired. Notice, he did not tell him that because he had been faithful to pursue him he would receive. He did not tell him that because of his asking he would receive. Rather, he told him that if he saw the chariots of fire and the horses of fire, he would be given what he desired. Basically, he told him there would be a "final exam" and, if he passed it, he would have what he desired. All of Elisha's faithfulness, commitment, loyalty, determination, and love did not insure he would receive the double portion. Those things certainly positioned him to receive, but it was seeing the horses and chariots of fire that allowed him to receive. Elisha could have made all the proper preliminary moves and still failed the final exam. He could have been denied the final impartation on the day Elijah was taken away.

All of Elisha's faithfulness to pursue allowed him to be in the position for God to impart to him his desire. God placed that desire in Elisha's heart, but it was Elisha's ability to see what was happening by the spirit that allowed him to receive the double portion of Elijah's anointing. When he saw the chariots and horses of fire, he saw into the spirit realm. He had the spiritual insight to see what God was doing and not simply what was taking place in the natural realm. He saw what God was saying in the situation, not what the enemy was saying. He had a heavenly perspective. This was the requirement Elijah had given him (2 Kings 2:10).

Throughout his journey with Elijah, Elisha was confronted many times by the "sons of the prophets" (2 Kings 2:3,5, NKJV). informing him that his master would be taken away. The sons of the prophets, I believe, represent those in training. They hear of things to come and see those things not everyone sees, but they have not fully learned to interpret and effectively handle what they hear and see. Elisha was wise to tell them to be quiet. Imagine what this knowledge could have caused had he chosen to listen. He may have grown anxious concerning his time left with Elijah and tried to hurry the impartation process. He may have responded in fear and begun to repeat what he heard. There are many possible scenarios. I am so thankful he persevered to the end in order to be in position to see and accurately interpret what God was doing. Why am I thankful? I am thankful, because he gave us the perfect picture of how God promotes. He trusts us with a greater level of operating in His power when we have shown we are more in tune with Him and what He is doing than with what people are saying and what circumstance exists in the present.

Elisha did not listen to the sons of the prophets, because the enemy found no selfish ambition in him. Selfish ambition would have caused him to be more concerned for himself and his future promotion opportunities than for his Master. He did not listen to the sons of the prophets, because the enemy found no self-promotion in him. Self-promotion would have led him to maneuver in his own understanding and strength for position. He did not listen to the sons of the prophets, because the enemy found no fear in him. Fear would have caused him to begin to look at the circumstances and worry about how it was going to affect him rather than continuing to trust God and walk with his mentor.

I am repeating this in order to bring to your conscious mind the times you have listened to the sons of the prophets, thereby allowing the information you received to drive you to action instead of allowing the Lord to work out circumstances in His perfect timing.

While some may think that Elisha was able to see the chariots of fire and the horses of fire because he had some supernatural gift for seeing into the spirit realm, I do not believe this to be the case. Rather, I believe God permitted Elisha to see, because he chose to listen to the voice of the Lord rather than the sons of the prophets. He passed the test, proving that his flesh would not respond to certain stimuli. He had to be more in tune to the truth than facts, and he was! It was because of Elisha's submission to God that proved his readiness to step into the position he was seeking. The double portion was not Elijah's to give or to keep; it belonged to the Lord. Because the Lord could trust him, he was allowed to see into the spirit realm. It was the Lord who made the decision. It is the Lord's mercy that keeps us from promotion when we are not able to pass this test. He is not punishing us, but rather protecting us.

The information that the sons of the prophets were giving to Elisha could have distracted him. Had he partaken of this knowledge, it would have broken his focus and changed the outcome. I believe he trusted God and maintained his course without interruption. He saw what the Lord wanted him to see, not what man was bringing to his attention. It is very important that you properly discern what to do with information that comes your way, especially at times of transition. I can promise you that the "sons of the prophets" will be very willing to feed you information that is tempting to your ears and strategically designed to break your focus. They are not aware of this. They are usually sincere. It is your test.

This is just one example of how wrongly interpreted circumstances can be a stumbling block to your pursuit of destiny. This is the pattern you will see without exception. When promotion is on the horizon, along will come the sons of the prophets—often with very sincere intentions—discerning and speaking to the situation. If you listen, you partake of death; if you resist, promotion is imminent. Everything in your flesh will scream to give attention to the information. You must, by the grace of God that is only given to the humble, overcome. Let this be the locator of what needs to be crucified. Lay it out to the Lord, repent, and get on with this wonderfully exciting journey of walking with Him and being His servant. If you have located a place where you allowed information to alter your focus, repent, determine what act was your weakness, and take it to the cross. He does not want to *heal* our weakness; He wants to *totally remove* our weakness. This is a great place for us to receive what the covenant provides and exchange our weakness for His great strength!

You can be assured you will have another opportunity to choose life. You will have another opportunity to ignore the sons of the prophets, better yet, to tell them to be quiet! You will have another opportunity to stand firm in your commitment to trust the Lord. I believe the following statement can revolutionize any Christian's life if they will truly believe it: There is no one—no person, no demon, no evil spirit, no demonized person, not Satan himself—on this earth who can stop what the Lord has for you except you! If you will trust Him, He will see to your promotion in His perfect time.

Promotion is certainly not the only situation in which offense surfaces. You will find it everywhere. It is a virus lying in wait to contaminate everything you will do for the Lord. He has not called us to walk free of its presence; He has called us to walk free of its effectiveness. We are called to be overcomers, not to live in a box of no resistance. To walk with God is to be resisted by the enemy with offense; you will not see one without the other. There is certainly a place to resist the enemy. This is a defensive weapon given to us as believers, but if that is the only weapon we use, we will be tied up constantly with resisting and usually pulled far off course.

The devil is a liar. He tells lies and facts contrary to God's truth. He will continue to resist the work of the Lord until his final sentencing. As a believer, you have authority over the works of the enemy. Walk in the knowledge of that authority given by Christ and pray that His followers will walk in covenant love. This is what I believe:

> If the body of Christ,
> Would not be so eager to listen to the enemy's
> accusations,
> Would be quick to believe the best,
> Would give persons the benefit of the doubt,
> And even if a wrong has been committed,
> Would confront in love,
> The enemy would not be able to bring so much strife and
> division.

He is doing it by the authority we are relinquishing to him! Ouch!

Let me offer a different perspective on betrayal. We have all experienced this hurtful act at differing levels and degrees. What we often do not realize is the enemy is not only trying to hurt the one betrayed, but also just as equally trying to damage the one doing the betraying. This is where true brotherly love can be put into action. When someone is coming against you, trust the Lord to protect you, and go into prayer for your brother or sister. Rarely do people betray one another knowingly; they truly have been deceived and believe they are justified in their behavior. In those times when an act of betrayal is deliberate, continue to pray for the person and trust the Lord to protect you. Acts of obedience are your only requirement.

There is no hurt quite like the betrayal from someone you trust, someone who has gone through many trying times with you and been allowed by the Lord to know your deeper fabric. In my own life I have experienced situations where it was not my enemies who believed things against me that were not true, but rather those of my closest circle. Through those situations, I came to experience the prayer we all at one time or another will have to pray if we are obedient: *Lord, forgive them.* If you will take the pain to the Lord and just begin to pour out your heart to the only one who can touch that pain, you may open your mouth wanting to say, "Lord, get 'em!" However, you will learn to pray, *Lord, forgive them. They don't understand what they are doing.* It in no way justifies their actions, but the Lord will give you a vantage point that only He can give. He will go on to assure you that He will take care of the situation. That realization will bring peace that will allow you to go on. Of course you will still hurt, but you will have peace, and you will be able to forgive and lay it down for the Lord's handling. You will be free.

When we refuse to give attention to the strategy of the enemy, we will overcome. To see you overcome thrills the heart of your Father. To overcome through covenant love is the qualifier for involvement in someone's life at a deeper level. Shun offense as if it were deadly, because it is. It ministers death.

As mentioned in the beginning of the chapter, we are simply instructed of the Lord to not be easily offended. Another way of saying this is to not be "touchy." It is time that the body of Jesus developed a tough hide, not being so sensitive to the actions of others. Hypersensitivity is a sign that healing needs to take place in your soul. If this is the case, seek healing and get on with the task of being a vessel of healing for others. It is simply time to forget about ourselves in favor of the needs of others, preferring others above ourselves. When our feelings have been hurt, we must seek the Lord. If His leading is to confront the person, then we must confront with the intent of winning a brother. In most instances though, we are to forgive and go on, giving very little attention to the incident.

I've heard it said, "I want to go where I am celebrated, not tolerated." The problem is that if we only go where we are celebrated, we will not be going to some of the ones who need what we have to give or have what we need to receive. Iron sharpens iron. We must come to appreciate being tolerated and recognize it for the great gift it is. We must purpose in our hearts that being celebrated is a luxury, not a requirement. It is wonderful to be celebrated, and the Lord will see to it that we have someone to celebrate us, but the truth of the matter is that many times we will be misunderstood, rejected, unappreciated, gossiped about, and ignored. If celebration is our requirement, we will accomplish precious little for the kingdom. If all the enemy has to do is use the fickle nature of humans to get you to walk away from your calling, you'll never stand faithful to you calling. Here's a guarantee: when you are obedient, the enemy will not have to look hard to find a vessel willing to cause you frustration. The Lord sends truth where it is needed. It is not usually wanted where it is needed, and where it is not wanted, it is initially rejected. We are not being rejected. It is either our flesh or the truth we carry that is being rejected. If it is our flesh, we are to allow the Lord to crucify it. If it is His truth, what a wonderful opportunity to share in the sufferings of Christ!

To be transformed in the likeness of Christ is an incredible miracle that only the Lord Himself can accomplish in us. It basically requires the laying down of our natural nature and the embracing of Christ's nature. We must be crucified with Christ if we are to reign with Him. We hear the word *crucifixion* so much that I believe we often fail to fully comprehend what is actually taking place. We are actually experiencing the death of our fallen nature through the process of crucifixion, which is a slow, painful, and humiliating death.

As we allow the Lord to do this work in our lives, the truth He brings is sometimes hard to handle, because it is very contrary to our natural nature and will at first offend us. When the flesh is offended, it will resist the truth and becomes stiff, stubborn, and prideful. Our mind will think of many excuses to justify our wrong behavior. What makes the behavior wrong is not that it cannot be justified by circumstances, but that it is contrary to the nature of God. When this is happening you usually find yourself justifying your actions with facts, feelings, and circumstances. You will probably find yourself becoming angry. When this happens with me, I can actually feel my physical body stiffen (Prov. 29:1). This resistance is rooted in pride. Stephen referred to the religious men of His day as stiff necks (Acts 7:51, KJV). There is just a real stiffness in us when we are resisting the truth. Another warning sign is that resisting God is very physically fatiguing. It will wear you out!

However, there is a very real attack of offense waged against us by the enemy. This attack can bruise and wound the spirit, and if undetected, can result in a spiritual wound causing retreat from the things of God. There is a type of suffering we do for Christ and there is another type of suffering the Lord has nothing to do with. There is an offense to the spirit that is very different than an offense to the flesh. This type of dart must be identified and handled differently. If the two are confused, we may find ourselves coming under bondage to an abusive situation where much damage can be done. I take the time to address this only briefly; it is further addressed in chapter 10. This subject deserves a book of its own, but for the sake of the reader who may be experiencing spiritual offense, I must try to clarify the difference.

Even though both attacks come from the enemy, offense to your flesh is designed to cause you to become angry and therefore separate yourself from others. This offense can be overcome by yielding to God through obedience to His Word. Offense to your spirit is designed to pervert your understanding of your heavenly Father. It is intended to cause you to back off of the truth you have learned. Forgiving and standing firm in the truth you know can overcome this type of offense.

The enemy cannot touch the born-again spirit, but he can assault your soul with accusation and intimidation. If you come into agreement with him, you will come to believe a lie. Remember, the enemy can only take from you what you are willing to relinquish. There is tremendous power in agreement, whether you are agreeing with God or with the enemy. If the enemy can get you to agree to a lie, you have relinquished to him your authority in that area. There are some who think they have done too much wrong for the Lord to forgive them. This is a lie, but it is a lie the enemy of our soul loves to tell. The enemy can only take from you what you relinquish in response to his attacks.

When you have been unfairly treated by another, do not come into agreement with the accusation. Immediately forgive the person, and pray for them. It does not matter how you feel. Just be obedient to the instruction of the Lord to pray and forgive. Simply stated, this means to leave the situation to the Lord for handling. Obedience will bring the blessing of God's protection. He alone is your defense. Leave the situation to Him.

If you handle this situation in obedience to the Lord's instruction to walk in love, it will not only preserve the jewels in your spirit, but will also allow the Lord to use the attack to purge any error that may exist alongside the good seed in your heart. What the enemy means for harm, the Lord will use to refine you as pure gold.

If you do not recognize what is happening and immediately forgive, you may receive the accusation as truth and allow condemnation to come upon you, altering your understanding of the nature of your God. At this point, you will feel condemnation and shame. When the Lord convicts, you feel corrected and loved. There is a clean feeling. When the enemy of your soul condemns, you will feel shame, which is an oppressed, heavy feeling. When the Lord is dealing with you, you will always have hope.

Another thing that may happen if you don't forgive is that you will attempt to protect yourself and judge the other person, opening yourself to judgment, unforgiveness, and eventually bitterness. If you fall into this trap and do not quickly repent, a root of bitterness will grow in your heart. The Bible tells us that this bitterness in our heart will cause many others to stumble. This is removed by submitting to the Lord's command to forgive and releasing it to Him.

If this wounding is coming through the existing leadership in your life, forgive and pray. Know that the Lord is a great protector. He will not allow you to continue to be harmed. Trust Him for direction. There may be times when we are under leadership that is harsh and unfair, but that does not mean the Lord has not placed us there. Saul was certainly the Lord's choice for David's development. We can rest knowing that wherever God places us, His hand of protection is near. It may be difficult, but it will always be beneficial. It is very clear that the Lord expects us to forbear for the good of the whole. Leaders are ordinary people and have their own areas of weakness. Be quick to forgive. Seek the Lord for understanding.

If the situation is abusive, the Lord will open a door for your exit in His perfect timing. Never leave out of fear or stay for comfort. Leave or stay out of obedience to the Lord. Fear cannot be an issue. Comfort cannot be an issue. When I was in college, I had professors I enjoyed and professors I did not enjoy. I learned from all of them. As a matter of fact, some of my most valuable lessons have been learned through those I did not particularly enjoy learning from. You are not assigned to a location because the leader is wonderful; you are not released because they are not. You are assigned and released according to the purposes of the Lord. He is the Commander in Chief, and it is best to move about in His timing and according to His assignment. The army of God is just that—an army. We do not randomly make decisions as to where we go and what we do. We certainly can make requests, but sometimes we are given assignments that are not easy. It is our job to be submissive and complete the task. Trust the Lord for His protection. You will be given a way out in His timing.

Just as we must learn to avoid being offended, we must be careful not to offend others. Let me share a story to illustrate a principle here. My college degree is in the area of education, specifically physical education. My student teaching class consisted of seventh- and eighth-grade girls. At this transition age, many changes are taking place in their bodies, and in the physical education class, teachers begin to discuss subjects such as hygiene, the use of deodorant, and so on.

There would be days, especially in the warm months, when body odor would require action on my part. Being sensitive to their feelings, I would dismiss class ten minutes early, announce that I noticed some people were forgetting their deodorant, and require that all students take a shower, wash well, and use deodorant. I would give them about five minutes and then make a surprise visit to the shower room. Typically, I would find the two or three girls who were creating the problem attempting to dress without taking a shower. The girls who were probably squeaky clean before ever getting into the shower were scrubbing their little bodies with great vigor. I realized quickly that the ones who needed the correction the least were the tender ones who were most certain I was speaking to them. They truly thought they might be the ones I was talking about.

It is this tendency that sets the stage for young, tender believers to be hurt in their spirit. When leadership attempts to correct a handful of people by directing their comments to the entire group, the tender ones are most sensitive to the correction. The ones needing the least conviction are usually the ones who are most easily convicted. When the darts are thrown, they don't just hit the intended target. They hit the tender, vulnerable, and trusting heart that is wide open. We are to be careful not to offend others. To deliver God's Word with judgment is impure and cannot be received in love, because it is not being delivered in love. Frustration delivered from the pulpit is being delivered with the gifting the Lord has given to powerfully deliver His Word. It will cut at the very heart of a person, and the ones most harmed are the tender ones. This may cause them to stumble, and we are not to cause the little ones to stumble. The Lord's Word is to correct, direct, and adjust in the spirit of love.

> But if anyone causes one of these little ones who trusts in me to lose faith, it would be better for that person to be thrown into the sea with a large millstone tied around the neck.
>
> —Matthew 18:6

Jesus loves us enough to correct us. He does not correct out of frustration and pain. He corrects from a heart to teach and restore. We are exhorted to do the same.

If you have been harmed in this way, forgive and pray. It is necessary for you to be in agreement with God's Word that says that the Lord is a shield about you and the lifter of your head. (See Ps. 3:3.) Your natural inclination will be to protect yourself; usually this will result in building a wall. This is another trap. You have one option in this situation—trust God's protection and continue to forgive. Never compromise truth. Continue to pray for the person. I promise you, the Lord will work it out and you will not be harmed. I did not say it would be comfortable, just that you will not be harmed. You will not be knocked off course. Walk in love; it is always the spiritual "antibiotic" to offense. Release the situation daily if necessary. Cast down every imagination against the truth of God's Word. God respects our free will. Things may not always work out the way you or the Lord would want, but if you will refuse to be offended and will continue to pray for the person, you will not be harmed. You will stay on course.

You have to know, no matter how much a situation hurts your heart, it hurts the heart of the Father more. No matter how much someone has hurt you, your heavenly Father loves them just as much as He loves you. His desire is for restoration. He loves you. Release it to Him.

Carryover Thoughts

- Offense will come regularly.
- The Lord will always speak to our hearts before He allows deception to come.
- We must be in tune to the ways of the Lord, not the circumstances.
- We must not only be careful to not be offended, we must also be careful to not offend.

Chapter 5

THE STUMBLING BLOCK OF THE FEAR OF MAN

> Fearing people is a dangerous trap, but to trust the Lord means safety.
>
> —Proverbs 29:25

It is impossible to fear the Lord and to fear man at the same time. Is fearing the Lord being afraid of God's wrath? To a degree, yes, but there is so much more to the meaning. Let's explore.

The Bible tells us that the fear of the Lord is to hate evil and hating evil is the beginning of wisdom. When we walk in a pure fear of the Lord we are walking on the path of safety He has provided. To venture off this path is often the result of fearing man, and that path, as we see in the Scripture reference above, promises trouble! It is not only unwise to fear man, it is sin, and for sin we don't need behavior modification, we need repentance. It is not an emotional issue where we need to make a change; it is a heart issue and the fruit of our unregenerate nature which only the Lord can change. The fast track to moving forward is repentance for wanting to please anyone, including ourselves, more than God. He calls anything we place above Him an idol. We are called to live for an audience of one!

The sin of fearing man will put you in direct opposition to the Lord and will result in decisions and actions contrary to His wisdom. You are operating in the fear of man when your concern for what man thinks and wants is greater than your concern for what the Lord thinks and wants. As His children, we are not to be afraid of Him, but we are to have a heart response the Bible calls the "fear of the Lord" (Prov. 8:13), a heart that loves Him so much we don't want to do anything to displease Him, not because we are afraid of Him, but because we love and reverance Him.

Let me give you an example from my life. I grew up in a conservative Christian family. From childhood I was taught about God the Father and Jesus. Little was spoken about the Holy Spirit. Consequently, I did not have a personal relationship with Jesus through the Holy Spirit. For me, Jesus lived somewhere far away and left guidelines we are to live by. I knew about Him, but I did not know Him. I had knowledge *of* Him, but I did not have relationship *with* Him.

My natural parents, on the other hand, I knew intimately. I not only knew about them, I knew them—their likes, dislikes, hopes, dreams, and desires. I was a very strong-willed child, but I did love my parents very much. As I grew older and entered college, many temptations were set before me. Growing up in the sixties in America, I was on the forefront of liberties being encouraged and values being challenged for the first time in the history of our country. Looking back, I am grateful for praying parents and grandparents as I know their prayers kept me from many of the influences so deceptively laying traps. However, as powerful as those prayers were, and as much as I know they were God's keeping power over my life, there was something else strongly influencing my actions. I had a pure fear of hurting my parents. Causing them disappointment and shame and bringing reproach on their name would hurt me more than being punished.

The consequences of rebellion were all around me—teen pregnancies, drug use, sad lives. There are so many consequences of sin. I knew if that were to happen to me, it would devastate my parents. I loved them and wanted them to be proud of me as their daughter. I knew it would break their hearts if I were to involve myself in some of the temptations before me. I had this mental picture of my daddy's brokenhearted face, and I could not bear to risk the chance of causing him such pain. The fear of hurting my parents gave me a standard for behavior and a motivation for obedience that worked as a restraining force in my life. They were the reins, so to speak, in my life that guided me.

Sin is very tempting, and there can be pleasure in sin for a season, so I did not refrain from many of these temptations simply because I knew they were wrong. I refrained, because I did not want to hurt my parents. I was much too young, immature, innocent, and, frankly, ignorant to fully understand the dangers and the subsequent consequences of disobedience. I did understand my love for my parents and my desire to not hurt or disappoint them. Although I made many foolish decisions, many were also wise, not because I had understanding, but because I was operating in a pure fear of my parents. This is how operating in the fear of the Lord will result in wise decisions we may not fully understand until much later. It is then that you understand why the fear of the Lord is the beginning of wisdom. It may not be until years later that you gain understanding.

This is how we are to fear the Lord. We are to be so sensitive to His heart that we would never want to disappoint or hurt Him. This comes by knowing Him, and if you truly know Jesus intimately, you will never want to hurt or disappoint Him. To know Him is to love Him; to love Him is to want to please Him; and to want to please Him is to fear Him.

To walk in the fear of man puts a hook in you, allowing the enemy to manipulate with such ease. There is certainly nothing wrong with wanting to please man, to offer help and assistance, to be a good friend to others. However, when our desire to please another causes us to do something against our values or standards or against an instruction the Lord has given, we have crossed a line and are allowing ourselves to be manipulated. When this occurs, we are walking in the fear of man, and fear of man is a guaranteed stumbling block!

It is crucial we receive and understand our instructions from the Lord, our Commander in Chief. Once we have received our instructions, it is equally important we carry them out according to His plan, not ours. If we fear man, put any trust in the arm of the flesh, and fail to totally trust in the Lord to bring things about in His timing and in His way, our enemy will see to it that there are many stumbling blocks thrown in our path.

To walk in the fear of the Lord provides protection. God is our Source and our Provider. He is our Comforter and our Friend. While He often uses man as His vessel for provision, we are to never look to man for what can only come from God. Man can have impure motives and may send unspoken threats of conditional support. The support can be emotional, physical, or financial. We must trust in our God, not in man, for all we need. Obedience to this commandment may bring negative consequences, and we must be willing to accept those consequences. As we know, obedience brings blessings, but sometimes it will first bring persecution. Between obedience and the reward, there may be a cost for a season. Actually, I believe it is more accurate to say, there is usually a cost for a season.

It is easy to recognize when someone is pressuring you to do something illegal, immoral, or against the Word of God. However, the enemy of your soul is very clever in his approach to bringing you into error. You are no match for him in your natural ability. Jesus defeated him on the cross, and it is only through that victory that you can stand against this temptation. He knows you are not going to fall into overt sin, so he will lay a trap using something that looks good. What makes it sin is that it is in direct opposition to what the Lord has instructed you to do. I have observed that the Lord will always speak the first word before temptation is allowed to come your way. Once He has spoken, I have found He rarely repeats Himself, but will bring to your remembrance what He has already spoken. It is your responsibility to walk in what He has told you. When you are confronted with an option, no matter how good it sounds, that is in direct conflict with what the Lord has already spoken, this should be a big red flag. This is the point where you turn away and in your heart you can hear Jesus speaking to Peter saying, “Get out of here, Satan” (Matt. 4:10). Jesus had just told Peter what was going to happen, and Peter with a sincere and genuine heart took a position which was in direct opposition to what the Father had spoken to Jesus. Make no mistake, Peter was being used of the enemy to present an option to Jesus with the intent of getting Him off course. We know this because Jesus did not respond to Peter. He responded to the one He knew was speaking! He responded by turning His back and not being willing to hear or entertain what was being presented. He resisted the influence of Satan, and the tempter had to flee! This is one of the most deceptive ways the enemy gets us off course, and, if undetected, you will find yourself wandering aimlessly down the road of detour shaking your head and not understanding where you are or how you landed there.

Here is a typical scenario: The Lord gives you an instruction, and you obediently go your way carrying out His command. Your vision is clear; your focus is fixed. Along comes an impressive person with a good idea designed to help many people. It may open the door for many opportunities of ministry. This person does not have knowledge of the instruction you have been given from the Lord. You realize their idea will take you in a different direction than the original instruction, but you believe you can do both. Maybe you did not hear clearly on the first instruction, or maybe the original instruction is for a later time. I do not need to list the unending number of rationalizations commonly used to justify disobedience. I can tell you this, the longer you contemplate the idea, the more confused you will become and the more likely you are to follow in the wrong direction. You seek council from those you respect, but you never mention the original instruction the Lord has given. You avoid and do not seek for counsel those to whom you have told the original instruction. When you avoid those who will remind you of something you don't want to hear, you have just been presented with the second red flag.

When you are seeking input from others and withhold the key element, such as an instruction from the Lord, you are not seeking godly council. You are seeking selfish encouragement. Unfortunately, there are precious few who will discern the snare and even fewer who will risk your relationship by telling you the truth. There is safety in a multitude of council, not a multitude of opinions and misguided encouragement. There is great danger in a multitude of opinions. You are being drawn away by your own lust and deceiving yourself. If you continue, you will begin to distance yourself from those people in your life who have knowledge of the missing piece of the puzzle, the original instruction. When you do this, you have deliberately avoided the Lord's warnings. Another word for this is *disobedience,* and it is at this point that your vision will become cloudy and your focus scattered.

This is the point where you must immediately slam on the brakes and regain focus, recognizing the temptation to alter your course. This will always require humility. The people with the good idea may have no idea how they are being used. They may be sincere, innocent, and ignorant of the plan in action. Their reaction is the best indicator of their motive. You must regain focus quickly, very quickly, because if you do not, the blinders come on the eyes, and the muffs on the ears, and you are foolishly navigating the road called "detour."

When this occurred in my life before, it was at this point that I could detect a small check in the pit of my stomach, as if there was something I needed to swallow and it wouldn't go down. This is where we need to throw on the brakes. Our concern may be that we will look foolish, double-minded, and unstable. We fear we will offend others and disappoint them, and because we are concerned about the way we look (because we are fearing man) we continue on with this lump in our throat. When this happens, we have opened a door larger than an overhead shipping door and invited a flood of distractions to enter our life, getting us involved with all kinds of good and wonderful things. They may be nice, sincere people. They may love you, but believe me, they do not have a clue what the Lord has instructed you to do, and you are so far off course and overwhelmed with busyness that you can no longer see clearly. The fog has rolled in, and your compass is on the floor.

You have attempted to assist God in His plan to bring things about and an Ishmael is on the way. Now this living and growing organism, for which you are responsible, must be given care. The nature of an Ishmael is they are jealous of what God births. They mock the child of promise. They bring strife and contention and are very high maintenance. They cause a stir in the atmosphere where peace cannot be felt. The Lord does not change His mind, and the alternate plans we devise will never be blessed by Him. Ishmaels of today are not people; they are the influence people may carry that is not in agreement with the plans of the Lord. What must leave is their agenda, not necessarily them. If your decisions are based on your concern for what they think of you or how they may retaliate if you do not agree with them, then you will not obey the Lord.

Abraham was required to lay both Ishmael and Isaac on the altar, just in different ways.

Always know you will be tempted with good ideas. What makes them not good for you is usually only one thing: they are in direct competition with the assignment you were given from the Lord. Although, there may be many motivating factors for allowing this path-altering distraction to come into your life, such as ambition, fear, impatience, and the like, the concern for how we will be perceived by man is usually part of the snare.

I wish I could tell you that by fearing God you will always be loved and everyone will understand. I so wish I could make that statement. What is more accurate, though, is you will suffer persecution, you will be misunderstood, and you will lose people in your life you thought were your friends. There is a price you will pay for being a servant of the Most High God.

There is so much talk about the price, as if it were hours and hours of prayer, days without food for fasting, and denial of the flesh to prove our love to our God. This is not and never has been the price we pay. These are acts of love to the one we serve. When did you ever fall in love and consider time spent with that person or meals missed because of that person a price you had to pay to be in relationship? Of course not! Heaven forbid! You did those things because you wanted to, because you were so "goo-goo eyed" over them you didn't notice that you had missed a meal or hadn't played a round of golf in two weeks or hadn't had a decent night's sleep in a while. These were simply behaviors that resulted from your passionate interest in another person. You did not go to your refrigerator feeling hungry and say, "I think I'll not eat today and maybe they will love me more." You did not eat, because you were so focused on them that you were not hungry. Certainly prayer and fasting are disciplines of the faith, and I in no way want to indicate they are not important. I just don't think they are the price you pay to be in God's army. They are the fruits in your life because of your love and commitment to Him.

The only price you pay for walking with the Lord is being misunderstood, persecuted, and made to suffer tribulation. You will be despised, rejected, abused, and accused. Do not fall into the trap of thinking you must pay the price of works. This will cause you to operate in works, which is the fruit of pride and guarantees you will be resisted by the very one you are trying to please. These works will be born of a heart of love and commitment to your Master. Works are not seeds by which we produce something. They are fruits by which we can observe something that has been produced within us. We can produce nothing of ourselves unless we abide in the vine of Christ, and it is by Him those works are produced in our life. That is why James said that his faith would be known by his works. (See James 2:18.) They are fruit, not some means to bring fruit about.

Let's recap. The price of serving the Lord and walking in obedience to His commands is not works of spiritual disciplines such as prayer, fasting, and sacrifice. These are all acts of love. The price the Lord promises is persecution and tribulation.

When you walk in the fear of man, you will withhold truth for fear of what others will think of you or for fear of offending them. When you do this, you have compromised your commitment to Christ and have fallen into a trap. Love and speak truth.

If your desire is to be loved and affirmed by everyone, you should not attempt to be a servant of the Lord, for a servant is not better than his master, and if Jesus was persecuted, you can be assured you will be persecuted too. This is not a job that comes with a popularity guarantee, but rather a persecution and tribulation guarantee. When you make the choice to walk in truth, everyone you come in contact with that has any extended dealings with you will eventually have two primary reactions. They will be attracted to you or repelled by you. For the Lord to position you, without it harming you, you must not be surprised by the reactions. Learn to expect them, and be obedient to take them to the Lord for His handling.

Carryover Thoughts

- You cannot fear man and the Lord at the same time.
- Fearing man is an internal hindrance that makes you vulnerable to manipulation.
- Obedience to the Lord's original instruction is better than any sacrifice. Ask Cain!
- Fearing man is the breeding bed for Ishmaels.
- Disobedience brings spiritual blindness.
- The price we pay to serve the Lord is to share in His sufferings.

Chapter 6

THE STUMBLING BLOCK OF FEAR

Do not fear anything except the Lord Almighty. He alone is the Holy One. If you fear him, you need fear nothing else. He will keep you safe.

—Isaiah 8:13–14

Then I heard a loud voice shouting across the heavens, "It has happened at last—the salvation and power and kingdom of our God, and the authority of his Christ! For the Accuser has been thrown down to earth—the one who accused our brothers and sisters before our God day and night. And they have defeated him because of the blood of the Lamb and because of their testimony. And they were not afraid to die. Rejoice, O heavens! And you who live in the heavens, rejoice! But terror will come on the earth and the sea. For the Devil has come down to you in great anger, and he knows that he has little time."

—Revelation 12:10–12

You have a God who loves you and has a plan to use you to advance His kingdom and carry His plan of salvation to the lost of this world. You have an enemy who hates your God and consequently hates you. He has a plan to stop you at every turn in fulfilling the plan God has for you. You have a God who has strategically plotted the path for you to be successful, and you have an enemy who will relentlessly war to do one thing. His mission is get you to take matters into your own hands, trust in your own abilities, and operate in methods inconsistent with the Lord's ways. He wants you to trust in yourself and not in your God. He does this through pressure, intimidation, and threats. The base emotion he exploits is fear. He will pressure you to do things out of fear of negative consequences. If you fear the things he threatens more than you fear the God you serve, then you will yield to his trickery. You will be like the bull in a pen with a ring in your nose and a heavy chain hanging from the ring. Your enemy will be able to jerk your chain and get you to do whatever it is he wants you to do. He will threaten your personal safety, reputation, success, comfort, advancement, provision, respect, and all the things we work so hard to attain. When he does this, if you do not trust God, you will yield.

Fear is a natural emotion the Lord has given to alert us to danger and prompt us to action. This is a healthy biological response to a natural warning system designed by God to protect us from physical danger. When we are threatened with danger, many biological changes occur in the body—the heart rate increases, respiration increases, and hormones are dumped in the blood stream designed to increase energy and alertness. When we experience the thoughts and emotions resulting from this natural occurrence, it is not an indication that we are operating in the fear that comes from not trusting God. This reaction is normal and natural. It is given for our protection. However, the fear designed to alter our course by altering our decisions is not natural, but spiritual, and is rooted in the heart condition of unbelief. You do not necessarily doubt God because you feel the physical emotion of fear. However, you are yielding to the sin of doubt and unbelief when you allow the physical emotion of fear to steer you from trusting the Lord and obeying His ways.

In the previous chapter, we discussed the fear of man. Although somewhat related, the stumbling block of fear operates very differently. The fear of man is a misplaced reverence to please; we esteem the approval of man above the approval of our God. It is motivated by our own need to have man's approval and is fueled by our desire to be esteemed by others. We are attempting to have something we want by carefully calculating our actions to achieve the desired result.

While the fear of man has us working for our popularity, the stumbling block of fear has us making decisions to avoid the threat of negative consequences. These threats are an attack waged by the enemy of our soul, specifically designed to speak directly to our mind or through other people and circumstances. If your enemy can find a weak point in your trust level in the Lord, he will relentlessly assault your peace and mess with your head. The answer is to let him find no area of doubt in you.

Your place of immunity is to trust your God

Trust is not something we can just wake up one day and have. It is built, and it is nurtured. We learn through ever-increasing degrees that we can trust. To trust someone we must know them, have history with them, and cast down thoughts and imaginations that would lead us to think contrary to what they have said is true. As believers, we must understand that we can trust our God, and His ways are the safest. One of the most dangerous places we will ever be is off course and out of His will for our lives. Conversely, the safest place on Earth is in the center of His will. To trust Him requires relationship, it also requires His grace, and that is only found in the place of obedience.

Make no mistake, our enemy knows our vulnerabilities and the areas where we lack trust in God, and these are the areas he targets. However, the problem is not the enemy; the problem is our lack of trust. Jesus did not come and say He will bind the enemy so he can no longer bother us. Jesus said that He has overcome the enemy and by faith and obedience to Him we will overcome too. Jesus said to Peter, "Peter, Satan desires to sift you like wheat, but I have prayed that you will overcome" (Luke 22:31–32, author's paraphrase). The Bible is clear in giving instructions on how to walk in the protection Jesus bought us. It is also clear that when life and death is set before us, we are to choose life. We have a choice. We can lean to our own understanding or we can acknowledge what God's Word instructs. God respects our decision. While it hurts His heart when the choices we make are not in our best interest, He will not override our will. It is sovereign to Him; it is a gift from Him, and He will not violate that will. Remember that we overcome by the blood of the Lamb and the word of our testimony. We are not to be afraid of the enemy's threats. While the enemy can be very convincing, we must always remember advice contrary to the Word of God is from the enemy. He is a liar and a deceiver, and he is out to kill, steal, and destroy us and all that is connected to us. There is a way that seems right to a man, but in the end it leads to death" (Prov. 14:12, NIV).

One of the most profound books that illustrates this principle is *The Gingerbread Man*. From the moment that foolish little gingerbread man jumped on the back of the fox, he was history. His fate was sealed! The fox knew he could not say to the little man, "You're toast! Go ahead and jump in my mouth now, because that is what will happen eventually." No, he did not say that. He brought him to his point of fate one little step at a time. While the option of jumping on the fox's tail was certainly the act that saved him at that point, the truth was it gave him only one place to go in the future, closer and closer to his moment of demise.

You can never trust a "fox" option. We all do it at times, and hopefully we all learn it is a mirage, a trap. In our walk with the Lord, when we have exercised a fox option, there is but one option left. That option does not include negotiations; it involves only one thing—repentance. True repentance brings deliverance. True repentance is not being sorry we're in our mess; it is being sorry we disobeyed our Father, simply because we love Him and want to please Him. Repentance brings deliverance and deliverance is when the Lord, out of His mercy, sovereignly takes you from the cage of the enemy. Fear is a prison with bars and chains. Jesus came to set the captives free. That is why the gospel is called the good news!

The enemy uses our natural nature to bring us into bondage. As he hurls his fear tactics our way, we usually feel powerless, angry, anxious, and confused. Our soul may feel stirred up, and there is generally a lack of peace. These are usually warning signs that you are being targeted with fear. Any or all of these and more can occur simultaneously. It will look as though no matter what you do, you cannot win. At this point you have two primary options. You can resist the thought and turn and pray, or you can give in to the pressure and take one more step on the fox's back. The battle waging before you is a battle between truth and facts. Your enemy will use facts to substantiate his accusations. See him as the attorney with horns. Your advocate, your attorney, is Jesus. He uses truth. Truth is the side we must always stand with, for it is the knowledge of the truth that causes us to walk in the freedom the Lord provides. Jesus is your attorney appointed by the Father. His Word is more powerful that any accusation by the prosecutor. Here is the very good news: *the Judge is your Father!* While this is all very true, and while this is all provided free of charge to you by what Jesus did on the cross, it must be received by you. You must believe and trust your advocate and your judge! While the love of God is unconditional, His provision of safety is not. To walk in the protection of the Lord we must walk in obedience to His Word.

The above picture is put in such simple terms, but to stand in the faith it requires is not always easy. It is possible by God's grace, but it is not always easy. Everything in the natural will attempt to move you from your position of trust. The enemy may be defeated, and his days are very numbered, but remember he has very little time. He is not going to give up without all the fight he can muster. There are difficult times when you commit yourself to walk in truth and to trust your God in the face of circumstances looking grim. The cost of walking in truth is quite often very high. There is always a great price to walking in truth and integrity. It is wonderful to pay that great price, because it is part of sharing in His suffering, and that equates to sharing in His reigning. If you will obey Him, if you will trust Him, you will be protected. It will not always be easy. There will be times you think you are mad. There will be times others may think you are mad, but you will be protected. You will come out on the other side. You will be saved. The Lord tells us He has not given us a spirit of fear, but of power and love and a sound mind. (See 2 Tim. 1:7.) When you trust Him you will be bold and have a loving perspective and clear understanding.

The best antidote for fear operating in your life is a strong knowledge of who your Lord is and a strong trust in His faithfulness. This is truly the simplest explanation of how to walk free of fear and intimidation. When you know your God and the power of His might, the commitment He has toward His own, and the faithfulness He always walks in, you cannot believe the threats of the enemy. There is an assurance and a confidence you will begin to walk in that will annoy some. When this occurs you must know they are frustrated because they are unable to find a weakness where they can snare you. You cannot trust your God and walk in fear at the same time.

There are words like *faith*, *fear*, and *love* that are connected in such a way that it is impossible to separate them when revealing this stumbling block. Faith is simply knowing who He is and truly believing He does what He says He will do. To doubt this opens the door to fear. To doubt the Lord is to not trust Him. He tells us faith works by love (Gal. 5:6), He is love (1 John 4:8), and perfect love casts out fear (1 John 4:18). If you know Him, you will love Him; if you love Him, you will walk in a holy, reverential fear of Him; and if you fear Him, you will not fear anything else above Him. It is not possible to believe two contradictory things at the same time. You cannot know God and His promises and then fear that He will not do what His Word has promised He will do. If you are in fear you do not completely trust Him, and if you do not completely trust Him you simply need to know Him more. You may know all about Him, but you cannot intimately know Him and doubt Him. There are some very specific promises He has given us. He cannot lie.

At this point we may want to stiffen up, suck it up, and just be strong! Again, that is not the answer. This is not something we can do in our own strength. The answer is not to toughen up and be strong. The answer is to know Him, and through this relationship, He will make you strong. His strength will operate through you. The same strength He had to go to the cross will be available to you. The same strength He had that allowed Him to stand against persecution, mockery, ridicule, rejection, and all sorts of insults, will be available to you. Paul said that where he was the weakest the Lord was the strongest (2 Cor. 12:10). Imagine that! As I pondered this one day it occurred to me that maybe He is the strongest in us where we know we are weak. This is probably because those areas where we know we are weak are also those areas where we do not have confidence in ourselves. Because of this lack of confidence we will lean on Him more. Therefore, the more we lean on Him, the more He is able to be strong in us. The bottom line is there is no strength in us that does not look pitifully weak compared to Him.

If you are going to fully reach your potential and become a victorious Christian, it will be absolutely necessary to know Him intimately. We minister from the overflow coming from our well—a well only the Lord can fill as we commune with Him and abide in Him. You will not be able to draw from a well of intimacy if you have not established a relationship with Him. You cannot give away something that you do not have. If fear is operating in your life, thank the Lord a weakness has been revealed, and begin to trust Him to strengthen you in that area. This is not a time for false security. There are some very specific signs indicating where we have fault lines. Fault lines will begin to show under pressure. So, deal with them now while the Lord is calling and then when the appointed time comes, you will be a source of strength for others in times of trials. Your purpose on this earth includes the privilege of being Jesus' extended hand to others. There is no greater reward and there is no greater feeling than to have His power flow through you to minister life and encouragement to another. There is nothing on this earth that can compare!

I remember many years ago when the Lord allowed me for the first time to carry a word of encouragement to someone. I had read a book that was quite a blessing to me personally. As I was reading I kept thinking it would bless someone that I knew. That is how subtle the Lord can speak to you. When I was finished, I gave the book to this person to read and simply said I thought they would be blessed by the message. A week later they came to me expressing how timely the book had been and how touched they were by the message. With no prior notice, I simply spoke a few words of encouragement. As I was speaking I could literally feel God's love flowing through me to this other person and their eyes filled with tears as the Lord was touching and comforting their heart. I had no idea of the particular circumstances I was addressing, but I knew they did, and I was so very grateful the Lord allowed me the privilege to carry this word of encouragement. As I walked away the energy and excitement I felt was unlike anything I had ever experienced. I could hardly contain myself. I wanted to jump and shout! It was greater than Christmas morning as a 5-year-old and greater than the best present I had ever received. I was hooked! As I drove home in my car I was just beaming and overjoyed and kept saying out loud, "Thank You, Lord. Oh, thank

You, Lord!" As clear as I have ever heard Him, He spoke this firm word of warning to my spirit, "Don't worship that!" It immediately stopped me in my tracks and I responded, "I won't, Lord! I won't, Lord! I promise, I won't, Lord!" It was many years before the Lord allowed me to do that again. He let me have just a little taste of things to come to see if I would be faithful to endure the training to handle His power with caution and reverential respect. He continued to develop me, prepare me, and try me to make sure I knew the source of the gift! There is nothing like walking in the intimate relationship He allows us to have with Him.

Fear will keep you from stepping into your God-ordained purpose. There is a great shaking in the earth today. External threats and fear are at an all-time high. This is a time for great vigilance and sobriety. Personally, I do not want to simply survive; I want to be a well others can draw from in this time of shaking. That is what I want for you. I believe you want that too, or you wouldn't be this far into the book. Don't try to figure out how you can gain more power, position, and influence. Don't try to figure out how you can preserve power, position, and influence. As a matter of fact, don't try to figure out anything. Just begin to spend time with the One who has all the answers—the One who has all power, all position, and all influence. It will be in that intimacy where you will gain the security needed in times when circumstances look very different from what the Lord tells us is the truth. He will never leave you; He will never forsake you. (See Heb. 13:5.) He is faithful, and He cannot lie.

I wish it were true that we will never suffer and will always have everything we want. This is just a teaching I cannot find supported in Scripture. Paul, in his words and in the stories recorded about his life, clearly tells us there will be times of little and there will be times of plenty, but in either case we are able to do all that is required of us by the strength and power given to us by Jesus (Phil. 4:12–13). The Lord tells us a servant is not better than his master, and if

He suffered, we are going to suffer too. (See John 15:20.) No, we don't have to pay the price for our sin. That is not a price we could ever pay, but we will share in His sufferings. He has promised us tribulation and persecution, but He has also promised to supply everything we need. (See Phil. 4:19.) The operative word here is *need*. Note that it does not say *want*. There will be times of plenty and there will be times of little, and it is in all these times we are to be content, knowing and trusting He will take care of us.

I believe there is a great time of harvest soon to come unlike the world has known in recent times. As you listen to many of the end-time prophecy teachers speaking today, there are many different views expressed as to how the church will navigate through what is referred to as a time of shaking. (See Hag. 2:6.) I have listened to many of these teachers, and yet many differ in how they perceive the small details of how the end-time events will unfold. While it is good to watch for the signs of the times and to be vigilant on our watch, this cannot be done at the expense of being prepared to do what God has destined each of us to do. We must get ready. We must be prepared to stand faithful in the face of difficulty. This endurance comes from allowing the Lord to train and strengthen you in the area of trusting Him. When you submit to this training, one of the first things it will purge is fear. There is a job He has for us to do. I want to do all He has called and prepared me to do, and I want that for you. More importantly, He wants that for you.

If the Lord has prepared His people for a great end-time harvest—if He has promised to reveal His glory on His church—it certainly sounds as though He has something great He is preparing us to do. It is very possible there are going to be some times of great tribulation where at the same time the church of Jesus Christ will walk in a greater outpouring of His power. He has promised a great outpouring of His Spirit. At this point, I believe we have only seen sprinkles of that outpouring. I love the Lord Jesus with all my heart and plan to spend eternity with Him, but I believe there is a job for all of us to do while we are here. Earth is not our home, but our life on this earth is a gift from Him. It is my personal opinion that if we could see the great cloud of witnesses that have gone before us, we would see the original apostles eagerly cheering us on and thinking what an awesome privilege it would be to be chosen to be on the earth at this time. They are in our corner, and they can see clearly and know our victory is secure if we stay in relation with the One who has already won the battle.

The Lord tells us to occupy until He comes (Luke 19:13, NKJV). He has a specific destiny for every person. I want us to fulfill our destiny before we leave this earth. We have been prepared as warriors. Warriors want to fight a war for the cause. We certainly have a cause, so let's prepare to fight. Our weapons are not bombs, guns, and arrows. They are love, prayer, and boldness given only by the Holy Spirit! Should the Lord come for me, I don't want to be in the corner somewhere, whipped and whimpering! I want to be looking up and fighting with His sword at the same time, each day increasing the number of people that will be saved. I want to be fighting the good fight of faith. I want to be like Nehemiah and his workers, refusing to stop building the wall, working with one hand and ready to grab their sword with the other (Neh. 4:17).

This is the heart of a warrior. Let this heart be in you, and if it is, there will be no room for fear. A lack of fear is not a death wish. It is careful adherence to the voice of the Lord and immediate obedience to His commands. This is your place of safety; this is your place of immunity. It must be purposed in your heart that no man can take your life when you are walking in the will of the Lord. You may lay it down, but no man can take it. Although Paul was martyred, it was not until after he finished his race.

If the element of fear is greater in our lives than the element of trust in our God, we will be held in check by our fear and we will not fulfill our destiny. Be bold, be strong, for the Lord your God is with you! (See Josh. 1:9.)

Carryover Thoughts

- The stumbling block of fear is not the physical emotion; it is allowing the threats of the enemy to intimidate you thereby keeping you from being obedient to the Lord.
- The most dangerous place you will ever be is out of the will of God.
- You cannot trust the Lord and be in fear at the same time.
- There is no room for fear in the heart of a warrior.

Chapter 7

THE STUMBLING BLOCK OF FALSE HUMILITY

> For who is God except the Lord? Who but our God is a solid rock? God arms me with strength; he has made my way safe. He makes me as surefooted as a deer, leading me safely along the mountain heights. He prepares me for battle; he strengthens me to draw a bow of bronze. You have given me the shield of your salvation. Your right hand supports me; your gentleness has made me great. You have made a wide path for my feet to keep them from slipping. I chased my enemies and caught them; I did not stop until they were conquered. I struck them down so they could not get up; they fell beneath my feet. You have armed me with strength for the battle; you have subdued my enemies under my feet.
>
> —Psalm 18:31–39

All you will do of value for the kingdom of God will be done by the grace of God. His ability operating through you is the only means by which you will be able to accomplish anything of value. The Bible teaches us that God gives grace to the humble and resists the proud. Therefore, it is accurate to say that only the humble will accomplish the purposes of the kingdom, because the purposes are only accomplished by His grace. Let us examine this virtue the Bible calls humility, because without it we will never fulfill our destiny.

What do you envision when you hear the word *humility*? Someone quiet, timid, and willing to always take the backseat in the car pool? A person who does not draw attention to themselves and only offers an opinion when called upon? Someone who would never presume they could accomplish a difficult task or display an attitude of confidence? Although we often interpret these characteristics as signs of humility, many times they are the fruit of timidity, fear, and self-focus. All of these are rooted in pride. Pride focuses on self; humility focuses on God. Pride is most aware of self's ability; humility is most aware of God's ability. So very narrow is the gate of humility, there is no room for self to enter.

To recognize the counterfeit is best done by knowing the real. In light of this, let us examine an incident in the life of someone the Bible clearly demonstrates was walking in humility. Let us examine the Bible story of David and Goliath found in 1 Samuel 17. How do we know David was walking in humility? He would not have been able to accomplish the defeat of Goliath without the grace of God, and God gives His grace to the humble.

We know the story. I pray as we recount the events you will see with new eyes.

The army of the people of God had been challenged for forty days by a heathen nation. A giant, over nine feet tall, called for a man to fight with him. The Hebrew nation was intimidated, frightened, and without direction. The young lad, David, arrived for the purpose of checking on his brothers and delivering food. As he approached he heard the threats of the Philistines and observed the response of the Israelites.

Without hesitation David confronted the situation, questioning the audacity of the giant. David's heart response was, "Who is this uncircumcised Philistine that he should defy the armies of the living God?" (1 Sam. 17:26, NIV). He knew his God and the power of His might. David was amazed at the arrogance of the giant to consider challenging the people of God. David began to confirm what had been promised by the king to the one who was able to defeat the giant, and he proceeded to assure the king of his ability to respond to the challenge.

Grasp the reality of what happened. An entire army of men was wringing their hands in fear, not knowing how to handle the threats of the giant. A young shepherd lad arrived, displaying indignation toward the enemy and confidence toward defeat. He displayed so much confidence that he convinced King Saul to allow him to fight.

This is not just a story; this is a true recount of a historical event. There really existed in history a young boy named David. There really existed a giant named Goliath, who was over nine feet tall. This is a true and factual story the Lord chose to include in the holy cannon of Scripture. It is God breathed and carries a message He desires us to learn from and use as an example for our instruction. This story has been told and taught since it happened. Let us examine how David must have appeared to his countrymen and to King Saul.

David was operating in an awesome assurance of God's ability, borne from his intimate relationship with Him. There was no room for doubt in the heart of this shepherd boy, who experienced many times the delivering power of the Lord in overwhelming situations. He did not wake up one day with the confidence in the Lord needed for such an awesome task. This confidence was borne of a relationship and many private incidences of protecting his sheep from lions and bears by the might of the Lord operating through him. David knew through experience the ability of his God and the faithfulness of His commitment on behalf of His children. He was operating in one of the purest examples of humility given to us in Scripture. He did not have confidence in his ability; he had confidence in God's ability to empower him. Rest assured, David had a great deal of confidence, and he did not hesitate to display that confidence. He did not feel it necessary to explain his confidence was in the Lord. He responded to the situation from the abundance of his heart without explanation. His focus was not on himself and how he was being perceived. His focus was on the situation at hand and how far it deviated from the truth of Gods nature. What David saw was not in line with what he knew to be true about the Father he knew so well. Out of the abundance of his heart came a response to what he was seeing. I believe he gave very little thought to his first words spoken.

When your reliance is solely in the Lord; when you know with Him you cannot fail; and when you know without Him you are sunk; you then are walking in humility. When you walk in this assurance, you will display a calm and a confidence that will sometimes be interpreted as either pride or stupidity. It will be interpreted as pride by those who recognize it and are envious they do not have it, and it will be interpreted as stupidity by those who do not yet know enough to recognize it.

When you withhold a heart response of boldness, fearing you will appear confident and full of pride, you are operating in false humility.

False humility causes one to back down from what they know to be the truth. It causes one to withhold their river and cover their candle. There may be many times as young disciples that we step out and operate in boldness, and we in fact are premature in our expression. But there must be room for this error. It is an open door opportunity for discipleship and is the responsibility of those more mature to help instruct in a spirit of gentleness.

It is not necessary to qualify all our actions with the statement, "Oh, it is not me. It is the Lord." I believe we often do this because we have been taught the importance of always giving the Lord the credit. Certainly this is very important, but this is done in the heart and not simply by the words we speak. There are many canned remarks we parrot because we think it is the appropriate response for the situation. The problem is that if we do not closely examine what is really in our hearts, we may be deceived into thinking we are operating from a position of humility when we actually may be operating in pride. The statement, "It is not me. It is the Lord," may put the focus on the person making the statement rather than the Lord. It draws attention to the person and their expression of humility. Our motivation for making this statement may be to insure we do not appear to be in pride. We may actually be taking pride in our humility!

When we are allowed to touch the lives of others by the leading and permission of the Holy Spirit, there will usually be a deep appreciation of us in the heart of the one being helped. This is a natural response, and it also gives the one being helped a focal point for expressing their appreciation. It is more important for us to be aware that we were allowed to be the vessel used by the Lord than it is to remind them that it is not us who deserves the credit. As vessels, if we can keep this proper perspective, our actions alone will be what God uses to instruct the ones being helped.

When receiving a compliment and expression of love, appreciation, and gratitude, it is better to respond with a sincere "Thank you," knowing in our heart it was the ability of the Lord that allowed us to succeed. We could go on to say, "What the Lord did through me, He can do through you." This puts the focus on the Lord's willingness to empower those who know Him and put their trust in Him.

Saying, "Oh, it was just the Lord," sounds humble, and it may be coming from a humble heart, but many times it is false humility. Even though we are saying the right words, our heart may be deceived into thinking we were the one responsible for the person's breakthrough. Just rest in the knowledge at this moment and let it forever be settled in your heart that any good thing we do for a person is because we have been allowed to be the messenger for the Lord and carry a piece of His heart. Without Him we have nothing of value to offer anyone. We do not have to help people; we get to help people. As we sit at the feet of Jesus, He will look down and say, "Take this message to Sally. Call Bill and tell him I love him and am praying for him today. Give Larry fifty dollars. His son needs a new pair of shoes." The possibilities of how the Lord desires to minister to His children through one another are endless. Walking with Him allows us to be His errand boy. That's all! When we begin to think we in some way can take credit, we have touched His glory!

When we truly know Him and by His grace are allowed to accomplish an otherwise impossible task, praise from man will only deepen our appreciation for the One who empowers us. The lions and the bears are the private victories only seen by a few people the Lord chooses to allow to know. He allows us to take down the giants in front of others. The lions and the bears of your life build character and deepen your trust in God. That is why, when we see a victory in someone's life and when we see a great giant fall to the ground, we can know there were many unseen victories leading to the big victory. We have to deal with the lions and the bears. We get to take out the giant.

Exaltation from man can bring pride; the exaltation from God, even if it is through man, brings humility. As we progress down the path of experiences, the Lord will, in His timing, give us the encouragement we so much want to hear. The key words here are *in His timing*. He will not feed our need to be constantly affirmed and approved by man. The need for approval by man or to receive praise from man will result in great droughts of encouragement from the Lord. As He chooses He may speak words of affirmation to our heart or have someone else speak His heart. Either way, if it is from Him, it will affirm in us a realization of His faithfulness and goodness. It will bring us to the realization of His goodness in spite of our weakness. It will place before us our ability compared to His ability and this realization will bring repentance on our part for thinking we could accomplish such a task on our own. This goodness of God produces repentance in us. Pride is forced out and humility pours in. Self-reliance pours out, and dependence on Him pours in. Confidence in ourselves pours out, and boldness and power pour in. I pray you have ears to hear!

I believe He desires to praise His children, encourage us, and let us know how much He loves us. We, on the other hand, may have a great deal of difficulty receiving praise from Him, either directly or through others, because we do not want to touch His glory. This is a common dilemma in the heart of the servant of the Lord, and the question will surface, "Lord, how can I reconcile my reluctance of receiving praise?" When this surfaces, it will trouble the warrior's heart, because they know this is a fruit of self-confidence and pride. However, they also know there have been many lions and bears, and they are stuffed and mounted on the wall of their heart. I believe this can best be answered as follows.

The Lord ordained and called us from the foundation of this world. As humans, there resided within us, in addition to our heavenly destiny, the impure nature from the seed of Adam. Consequently, most of us resisted the Lord much of the way in His early dealings with us. It has been His choosing us and pursuing us that has worked in us. Left to our own choices we do not have the nature to pursue Him. He did not draw us because we deserved it, but rather because of His love for us. We have not been called and prepared because of us, but in spite of us. We can take no credit because without the fruit of long-suffering on the Lord's part, we would never choose life. As we grow in our knowledge of Him, His wonderful love, faithfulness, and kindness, we will begin to yield to Him more, and the journey will become easier as He molds us into His image. We did not deserve it, but He loved us enough to pursue us anyway. Whatever success we are enjoying today, we can rest in the knowledge that it is because the Lord did not give up on us. We are permitted to step into a place or position because the Lord never gave up on us, not because we did so many things right. Many of us go kicking and screaming much of the way. He pursues us, endures our struggle, and keeps us by His hand. He is very pleased with us, not because we have done so many things right, but because even in our fallen nature we continued to choose life at our times of testing. Once we have understanding at a certain level, we will be given the opportunity to choose as the Lord has instructed us. Our only requirement is obedience. At this point He pursues us a little farther. He loves us in obedience to His law of love. He is the one who is faithful to complete the work in us.

Once we have the understanding that we are where we are in spite of ourselves, instead of because of ourselves, we can begin to walk in a greater level of humility, and the Lord will begin to supply us with a greater abundance of His ability. When our confidence is strongly rooted in Him, we will begin to operate in a higher level of faith and therefore a greater dimension of His power. This demonstrates the difficulty of separating faith, love, humility, and power. Where you see one there will always be the presence of the others somewhere in the background.

Our part is to not reject Him but rather embrace His dealings into our lives. More of Him will result in less of you. Simply striving for less of you will result in less of you but not necessarily more of Him. If you have a glass of dirty water, you can begin to dip out the water, spoonful by spoonful. When you have finished you will have an empty glass with some dirty water residue at the bottom. The glass will be empty. If you take the same glass of dirty water, ignore its contents, and simply begin to pour in pure, clear water, eventually it will purge the dirty contents from the glass. Through intimate relationship you are allowing the Lord to pour in the water of His Word and presence. As it floods your soul it will take care of the unwanted contents. This principle bears repeating because we so often get this backwards, and we try so hard through striving to be only what the Lord by His grace can make us. By allowing the Lord to pour over our soul, humility will come because He is humble by nature. Put this picture in your mind. It is a religious spirit, using doctrines of works, that instructs you to dip out the dirty water. It is the Holy Spirit that tells you to pour in the pure water. Focus on the Lord.

This is how we can know if we are operating from a heart of humility or pride. These two opposing heart responses have specific fruits, and we are instructed to examine the fruit. The Lord's grace is tangible in the lives of those walking in humility. David was certainly confident in the Lord's ability to overcome the giant. The fruit of David's humility was not only what he said, but also what he accomplished. He could only accomplish the victory with the Lord's ability operating through him, which is the fruit of humility. His brothers accused him of having pride in his heart. Actually, they were the proud ones, because they were looking to their own abilities to fight the giant. Always remember to look at the fruit. If there is humility, there will be grace, the Lord's intervention, ability, and favor in the situation. If there is pride, there will be no power to overcome. If there is no fruit, it usually means much is going on deep within us. No fruit is not necessarily bad fruit; it is just no fruit. Seed, time, and harvest have a timetable we cannot control, and the good news is every winter season is followed by spring. In the spring, smells are fresh, colors are bright, and life springs forth all around us. This is the same in the spring season of our walk with the Lord. Rest in knowing the Lord is doing much work in those times of dryness. If you love Him and yield to trust Him, He is working on your behalf, no matter what it may feel like or what it looks like. Trust Him!

Remember this: We can of ourselves do nothing; with His ability we cannot be defeated. However, He is not obligated to fight any battle we choose to fight. He will fight the battles He leads us into. When He has lead you into a battle and you have a resolve of heart, without question knowing and believing in the power of your God, you cannot be defeated. It does not matter what it looks like. There may be circumstances making a statement to the contrary. They are not the truth. If we are in His will, we cannot be defeated. Submitting to His will is an act of humility. Humility brings His grace. Humility brings His ability.

Humility is not feeling lowly. It is recognizing that we walk in an awesome power. Humility is not feeling a lack of confidence; it is recognizing we walk in an awesome confidence. Not in ourselves, but in our God. It is realizing we can trust the One who has all power and confidence in any situation He leads us into.

Was David quiet and hesitant to display his confidence? Hardly!

Was he timid, trying not to draw attention to himself? I don't think so!

Did he strongly communicate his desire to perform this difficult task with confidence? Apparently so. So much so he convinced King Saul to let him pursue the battle.

What was the response of his brothers? They probably said, "Who do you think you are?"

How must David have felt when he was accused of having pride in his heart? Certainly the accusation was intended to take his focus from the task at hand and put that focus on him. The enemy of your soul always comes on the scene to derail the plan of God and silence the word of the Lord. He will use anyone willing to yield to his accusation. When we listen and believe the accuser of the brethren, we become a door he can work through to hinder God's plans. Using the lack of respect toward their brother and through intimidation and manipulation, he used David's brothers to throw a stumbling block at David's feet. If this enemy of our soul finds a weakness in character, we will be targeted in that area of weakness. Praise God, it could find no weakness in David!

David had obviously overcome the stumbling block of fear; otherwise he would not have wanted to fight the giant in the first place.

He had obviously overcome the stumbling block of the fear of man; otherwise this accusation would have caused him to become more concerned with how he was being perceived and what others were thinking of him. He would have become concerned with his reputation. He would have become self-focused. The enemy will always try to get your eyes off your God and onto yourself or the situation.

He had obviously overcome the temptation of taking offense. I am certain the lack of support and understanding from David's family discouraged him. It may have bothered him, but it did not stop him.

Every time you come to a point of standing in the confidence of your Lord, the enemy will look you in the face and say, "Who do you think you are?" He will move on a vessel to be a mouthpiece, but remember, if he cannot find a vessel, he will accuse you to yourself and speak directly to your mind. Your answer, when you are asked who you are, must always be, "I am in Him."

All David wanted to know was, "What will a man get for killing this Philistine and putting an end to his abuse of Israel?" (1 Sam. 17:26). Imagine what some in the church of today might say about that. He would probably be accused of only wanting to get something in return. Actually, his question was just another indication of his confidence in his God. David was not deterred by the accusation but rather proceeded to knock Goliath off his feet and then cut off his head with the giant's own sword. But wait, he wasn't finished. He dragged the head around for a few days and then impaled it on a post near the gate to the city for all to see. (See 1 Sam. 17:54.) David was not saying, "Look what I did." David was saying, "Look what happens to someone who will dare to defy the Lord." His boldness, confidence, and strength were all fruits of his intimate relationship with the living God and his unyielding confidence in the One he knew to be with him. They were a fruit of his heart, a heart after God's own heart!

Simply stated, humility is having an unyielding confidence in and a total dependence on the Lord's ability. Pride is having confidence in and dependence on anything other than the Lord. Jesus plus nothing is always enough. Jesus plus anything is never enough. We cannot say we trust in Jesus and then go down into Egypt for our help. We cannot say we trust in Jesus and rely on the arm of the flesh. (See Isa. 31.) We do not have to have anything from anybody to accomplish what the Lord has for us to do. This certainly does not mean we do not need people. The Lord uses people and sets up situations where we are divinely connected with others for His purposes, but when we alter what we know we are to do because we are afraid we will lose the support of someone, we have altered our course. We do not need whatever they have that badly. Let it go. God can get it to you in another way.

David refused to accept Saul's armor. He had been preparing his entire life to face the giant on that particular day. The encounter was no surprise to the Lord. He set up the whole incident. Had there been one shred of doubt in David's heart, he would have taken Saul's advice. I do not believe he would have been successful if that had been the case.

We easily recognize pride when one is leaning on their own understanding and ability. What is harder to discern is the one that has no confidence in himself, and because of this, he will not step out trusting the Lord to be with him. This is usually interpreted as humility. It is not humility. It is pride. It is pride because the person is still looking to himself for the answers, not relying on and trusting in the ability of God to operate through them. It is false humility.

The stumbling block of false humility will hold you in bondage. It will cause you to be powerless, and it will keep you from stepping out in the things the Lord has for you to do. It will hold you between the place of knowing in your heart what you are to do, and yet being afraid you will appear overconfident. It is absolutely necessary this yoke of bondage over the minds of God's people be broken and shattered if we are going to function as the warriors He has called us to be.

I am so blessed to have been trained by the very best. I am one of those saints who received much training in "Egypt." Some of that is because I was not walking with the Lord and not pursuing Him within the traditional arena of church and Bible school. However, even in my rebellion, He led me into situations I have now come to realize were His choice training ground. Early in my personal career path I worked for a governmental agency that regulated employee safety. This type of work will quickly give you an understanding of the power a law carries and the hate you receive from those who do not like the law. It was a great picture of how we will be disliked by some people, not because of us, but because of who or what we represent. I did not realize the Lord was toughening my hide, but I can tell you it was safer ground than some of the church experiences I have had.

Later, I advanced to a job in private industry and was given responsibility for ensuring compliance with these same safety standards. It was at that time I had the absolute divine privilege of working for someone I believe was the greatest picture of how our Jesus backs us up as we work for Him. Certainly, I did not realize at the time what the Lord was teaching me. It took time for me to realize the value of the education and training I was receiving. I share this story because it draws so many perfect parallels to how the Lord has prepared a way to ensure our success at raising His standards and how He backs us up in all we do in compliance to His ways and directives.

When I met the person in charge of the entire division for which I worked, he introduced himself to me simply by the name Rip. He was a man of pleasant social graces, an intense and unyielding commitment to excellence, and a firm command. He wanted things done only one way—perfectly. There was never any doubt as to where he stood on an issue and what was expected of those under his authority. He said what he meant and he meant what he said. His position never changed.

Upon being introduced to him, he began to explain to me the responsibility of my position. He informed me his door was always open and that I had direct line access at any time. There were actually two management levels between my position and his, however, I was allowed direct access because my area of responsibility involved the safety of the employees. This man further assembled all the management members and proceeded to introduce me in the following manner: He informed them of the position I would be assuming and clearly communicated to them my direct line access to his office or home any day or hour. He clearly and firmly stated my presence on the production floor was to be viewed the same as if he were on the floor, and whatever I said was to be responded to as if he had made the statement personally. He made it very clear that I walked in 100 percent of his authority in matters pertaining to my area of responsibility. I was clearly given authority commensurate with the responsibility of my position.

The man I replaced was a well-built former Marine. I was 28 years of age but looked much younger. When I first met my predecessor, I could not even imagine how I was going to be taken seriously in this new position. I fought a great deal of doubt internally. What a beautiful picture of how Jesus backs up His servants! You see, when I walked onto the production floor, it did not matter what I looked like, my size or my stature. What mattered was whom I represented. Can you imagine how easy it was for me to do my job? It was so easy, because I was not walking in my own authority but the authority of the commander in chief of the plant. I will forever be grateful to this wonderful leader, for he was handpicked by the Lord to teach me a powerful lesson in the power of delegated authority. He will forever have my respect and appreciation, and I know there is a reward for him in heaven.

Unfortunately I learned the perils of walking without authority through the same channel. Rip was later removed from his position, because his style of management was considered to be too authoritarian and dictatorial. When he walked out of the plant for the last time, he took with him the commitment to excellence pertaining to the areas for which I had responsibility. My authority was removed. I no longer carried the mantle he passed on to me, and I learned very quickly what it feels like to have someone say, "Rip, I know, but who are you?" What a sad picture. What an awesome lesson! Our Lord's authority can never be removed, and He has delegated to us what we need to perform what He has called us to perform. Rest in the knowledge He will never leave you nor forsake you. He can never be stripped of His authority. There is none higher. He is the Most High God forever and ever. Amen!

David knew whose authority he walked in, and it was this realization that allowed him to walk in such humility. We do not have to prove anything when we know we have the goods. It is not because of us, but because of the one we work for. It is not because we cause anyone to fear, but because the one we work for causes demons to tremble. Jesus sends us in His authority. He has given to us all authority in heaven and on Earth.

When you are walking in accordance to His Word and His will—when you are operating within your specific job assignment—you can be assured He will back you up. It would not have been wise for me to attempt to tell the engineering department how to design equipment or the production department how to produce their product. That was not within the scope of my responsibility. It is important we know our place and stay in our place. The Lord will always give you the authority to carry out your responsibility. If you are lacking in authority, it is very possible you are outside your assignment. Warriors have many different assignments. It is important we seek the Lord for guidelines of our sphere of influence and responsibility. Not everyone can be in a position of high visibility, but make no mistake, if you are not in your proper position and functioning in your proper assignment, it will hurt the whole body. Each position is of great value.

Humility is not an action; it is a heart condition resulting in actions. If we truly do not understand the nature of this virtue, we will be hindered and taken off course. We may even think we are being obedient to behave in a way the Lord did not model and His servants did not display in their times of trial, testing, and victory.

It is not necessarily humility to be quiet and give someone a chance to speak their heart and share what they desire to share. This may be good manners, and it will certainly help your relationships and personal image, but it is not necessarily humility. Humility is a condition of heart, where you love the Lord to such a degree that you spend intimate hours with Him. Through this intimacy you grow to know His voice and recognize it when He begins to speak. As others desire to talk and share their hearts, you will then recognize if your Jesus is talking through them or allowing you to enjoy them through His eyes. He may allow you to speak His heart and encourage, exhort, correct, direct, and rightly divide. He may direct you to stop them from talking. As you acquiesce in respect to your Lord, you will be obedient to whatever He instructs. This is totally trusting and leaning on Him, depending on Him for direction and understanding. This is humility.

To patiently give someone equal time, thinking a humble person does not monopolize the conversation, is not necessarily humility. It is the act of being polite. That is not a bad behavior, but don't be fooled into thinking you are being humble, especially if you are not truly listening to what the person is saying. Much of what the Lord desires to give us through others is heard but not received because we cannot look beyond the wrapping on the package. This was true in the case of Jesus, and it remains true today. Intimately knowing the Lord allows us to recognize Him, no matter how He is packaged. It allows us to receive His direction, instruction, and affirmation through whatever means He chooses to get it to us. His sheep truly do know His voice.

Humility is placing value on others, as the Lord does. It is esteeming others to the degree the Lord esteems them. It is knowing people by the spirit and responding accordingly. The Lord not only has a way of making us feel important, He really does believe we are important. He not only has a way of making us feel loved; He truly does love us. He would never fail to address and thereby encourage us in behavior displeasing to Him. He loves us enough to disagree with us when we are in error. He corrects us when we misunderstand. He tends us like a good shepherd, and He laid His life down for us.

At the heart of true godly humility is a true sincerity that cannot be duplicated in any other way. It is the Lord's heart overpowering our hearts as we yield to Him. It is forgetting our reaction and yielding to His reaction. Any attempt to perform acceptable behavior on His behalf but independent of His heart is counterfeit. It is false, and it stinks in the nostrils of a holy God. It is false humility. Represent Him with His heart.

It is absolutely necessary to balance this chapter with chapter 10 on submission and authority. Now that you have hopefully received a greater freedom in the area of expression, let us remember the principles of balancing this expression with the proper submission to authority. We have removed a weight, but it is necessary we tighten the bit and reigns.

Carryover Thoughts

- The gate of humility is too narrow for self.
- Humility is not actions; it is a condition of heart resulting in actions.
- Humility is absolute trust in God.
- Humility focuses on God. Pride focuses on self.

- False humility is more concerned with appearing humble.
- True humility will draw accusations of being proud.

Chapter 8

THE STUMBLING BLOCK OF ABILITY

> Are you called to be a speaker? Then speak as though God himself were speaking through you. Are you called to help others? Do it with all the strength and energy that God supplies. Then God will be given glory in everything through Jesus Christ. All glory and power belong to him forever and ever. Amen.
>
> —1 Peter 4:11

The human being is fearfully and wonderfully made. It is hard to imagine what we must have been like prior to the Fall, and yet residing within each of us are remnants of that original glorious creation. I remember one occasion watching an ice skater perform to a beautiful melody. The artistic expression of both the dancer and the songwriter originated only from a gift planted in them by God. The graceful movement and beauty of the body accompanied by the music originated only from the one having creative powers. I experienced an overwhelming appreciation for God's creation. He has placed within all of us His gifts and talents and He has a desire and a plan for each of us to use those talents for His glory.

We may respond to His plan with rebellion and go our own way, choosing to use our gifts for our own gain and purposes. Sadly this occurs often and individuals who choose to take the path of self never find the peace, joy, and fulfillment the gift was intended to bring to them or others. This chapter is not intended, however, for those who are running from the Lord-ordained call on their lives and assuming ownership of their gifts. This chapter is for the individual who has made a decision to serve the Lord with their gifts and talents. When they recognize they have been entrusted with these special attributes for His purposes, they desire to fulfill that purpose. This begins a journey along the road of preparation, and this road promises challenges and surprises.

It may be hard to understand, but the very attributes the Lord has placed within us for our assignment can become the very stumbling block keeping us from fulfilling our destiny. How is this possible? I believe if you are reading this book, it is not because you are trying to decide whether or not you will yield your life to the lordship of Jesus. I believe you expressed that desire long ago. Yielding to His lordship means we give Him our lives. We give Him our dreams, and we give Him control of those attributes He has given us. As we do this He is allowed to take the abilities and gifts placed within us by Him and prepare us as vessels of honor for His purposes. This process requires much yielding to His ways and much dying to our personal dreams and plans.

We may think the Lord wants to take the abilities placed within us and perfect them for His purposes. While in a sense this is true, I believe there is a higher vantage point that more clearly illustrates His desire for our development. The Lord has made us in His image, and He has offered us a covenant relationship where all He is can be available to us. He is not trying to perfect us; He is the perfect one. The abilities He has given us in the natural are a shadow of what we have been called to do, and they are an indicator of how He desires to operate through us. God is a God of precision and excellence. Our gifts indicate how He desires to flow through our vessel, but once He has developed and refined the skill level within our natural abilities, He then asks us to lay them at His feet.

As we seek Him, He places within our heart desires for how we will serve Him by using our gifts. These desires may be to serve in business, entertainment, ministry, or many other areas where God chooses to plant those who are His. The day will come when we have completed the refining process to the point those desires can be given to us. All we have been prepared to do—all we have been waiting for—is placed before us, and it looks as though we have experienced the fulfillment of our promise. Our Isaac has been born, and we are allowed to enjoy this child of promise for a short season of time.

The spiritual yielding Abraham had to do with his son will be required of each of us as we begin to step into our position of promise. It is a principle of the kingdom; the Lord is never finished working in us. There are seasons of rest, but He is never finished. To be His servant is to continually be before His hand, allowing Him to make adjustments of preparation. Once we have been given the promise we are required to return the promise to the Lord. We must be willing to lay down all we have been given and all we have been promised—our dreams, hopes, desires, plans, and understanding. We sacrifice everything, not knowing how the Lord is going to redeem the situation. He is faithful, and He fulfills His promises, but we do not have the mental capability to understand how the Lord will do this. We must yield to His ways and be willing to trust Him in all things, allowing Him to control His mission. No matter what we have been given to do for the Lord, it is very important we understand it is His mission. It is not our mission.

He can only trust you with what you are willing to return to Him

Too often the Lord is allowed into our lives to the point of refining us for our assignment, only to hear us say, "Thank You,

Lord. I can handle things from here." We stop at the birth of Isaac, never allowing the promise to be laid on the altar. In this state, we have not submitted to His lordship. We are operating our plan expecting the Lord to bless our mission. He never will!

The pride of the human heart is incredibly deceptive. This is not a battle that can be won once, forever to be final. Self-reliance is to the human soul as weeds are to a garden. They crop up out of nowhere. Constant attention must be given to insure we are continuing to lean not to our own understanding, always depending on the Lord for direction and understanding. It can be viewed as an artichoke—no matter how many layers you peel, there always seems to be another. There is a realization and a yielding that must come in the area of our ability, and if we are able to make this adjustment, we will walk in obedience to the Lord's plans. We must come to the realization that our abilities, as our own righteousness, are as filthy rags compared to the ability of the Lord. He has called us to walk in His ability, not our own ability. We are offered the privilege of relinquishing what we have to take what He has. This is an incredibly generous offer, and yet the blindness of the human heart wants to hang on to our filthy rags. It makes no sense, but we are so blind to the trade He is offering that we hang on to what we believe are our possessions, not being willing to lay them on the altar of the Lord. If we can yield in obedience to His ways, what He will give us back is far greater.

The Lord needs nothing we have. He has everything He needs and desires to share it with His family. He does not need our brilliance. He is all brilliance. He does not need our creativity; He created the universe and beyond. He does not need our ideas; He is the Creator of all and wants to give us His ideas. He does not need us to help Him. His desire is for us to get out of His way so He may work through us to help others.

There is an alter where He wants us to place all we are, all we have, all we desire, and all we hope for. Return to Him whatever the Lord has given you in the area of ability and talent. Give Him your limited ability, and put yourself in position for Him to operate through you in His ability.

It is easy in the beginning to give the Lord all we have, because we view it as so little. When the turf is unfamiliar and our experience is limited, it is easy for us to operate in dependence on Him. However, as we progress in our development, in our own eyes we may mistakenly assume we are responsible for our success. At this point our heart attitude may become less dependent on the Lord and more reliant on ourselves. We will not say this, we will not even allow ourselves to think this consciously, but the fruits of our actions nevertheless reveal this to be what is in our heart. False humility will insure we verbalize our desire to seek the Lord and our desire to be lead by Him. Unfortunately actions are saying, "Thank You, Lord. I can take it from here." This is why Jesus said it was harder for a rich man to enter heaven. The more we have in the natural, the harder it is for us to realize how poor in spirit we really are. A person who relies on their own ability and has confidence in their own methods has simply forgotten what was actually accomplished by the miracle of salvation.

I am so convinced we are seeing only a trickle of His awesome miracle-working power because we are trusting in our own ability and understanding. The soul of man, working in absolute rebellion to the living God, is able to achieve great accomplishments, because, even in our fallen state, we are incredible creations. Natural methods can certainly produce results, but when our trust is in the methods and not in the Lord, the outcome will not be as good.

In Luke chapter 5, Jesus taught from one of the fishing boats. When He finished He told Peter to go out where it is deeper and let down his nets. Peter was reluctant, because he had been fishing all night without catching anything. Out of respect he did as Jesus instructed. Immediately the catch was so large the nets began to break. The catch was so bountiful they had to call for help.

What was the difference? Obviously, Peter was a skilled fisherman; it was how he earned his living. He had the necessary equipment and had worked very hard all night to catch fish. He was equipped, prepared, and hard working. When the Lord instructed him to try again, the only difference was he cast his nets where and when the Lord instructed. The results were bountiful compared to the result he had when he was leaning to his own understanding. While the Lord may have us use very natural methods, He can save us hours of time and energy if we will seek Him for guidance. However, if we have allowed the Lord to refine our abilities and have stepped into a role of influence, and yet have not placed those abilities in His hands, we are operating from our soul. We are leaning to our own understanding. We are being tripped up on our own ability.

In the area of ministry, if you are an encourager, then you will be able to encourage someone simply from your gift to encourage. If you are not seeking the Lord for guidance, you may be encouraging them in something that is not God's will for their life. There are times when people will try and pull something from you that the Lord has not given you for them. I believe when we are desperately dependent on the Lord for what we are to give His children, He is faithful to give exactly what is needed at exactly the right time. When we desire to be used of the Lord as His extended hand, we must trust and rely on Him for what a person needs. There is an integrity we must walk in that relinquishes the control of our gift to the Lord. When we are able to do this, He calls us faithful.

Unfortunately sometimes when we do this others may call us unfaithful, because we will not give them what they want. Always remember that as a servant you have ownership of nothing. Be faithful to only move with permission. When He gives you that green light, then speak what you believe the Lord has placed in your heart. When we speak what the Lord is saying to our hearts, He is actually borrowing our voice to speak His words, and He watches over "His" word to perform it, not over our words. His word in our mouths is what makes creative miracles. His word in our mouth will literally change the atmosphere in a room.

In the area of ministry it is always safe to encourage someone that the Lord is faithful, that His Word is true, and that no matter what they are going through, the Lord can make a way. We may always encourage others to seek the Lord and to trust He will guide them. These are unyielding and forever-applicable words of encouragement. We must never tell someone the Lord is going to bring them a husband, find them a job, or launch them into a ministry just because that is what they desire. We can only give people what the Lord gives us, not what they want.

I have had this situation occur many times in my life. On one occasion a very dear friend believed that she was to sell her home and move to another state to become a part of another ministry. While this was something the Lord had not spoken with me about, I knew she was a woman of prayer, and I trusted that she had prayed for God's guidance and direction on this decision. To be honest I always had an uneasy feeling about the move, but I would simply pray and ask the Lord to protect her and to pave the way for where He was calling her to be. Months passed and her house would not sell, even though she lived in an area so desirable that houses stayed on the market sometimes only hours. My uneasy feeling about her moving was increasing daily and the fact that her house was not selling was another indicator to me that possibly this was not the right move or the right time for her. One particular day she called specifically to request that I agree with her in prayer that her house would sell. I had not mentioned any of my reservations concerning her move, but at that point I could not tell her I would pray for God to sell her house! I simply told her I could not pray for her house to sell, but I would certainly agree with her in prayer that her move would be in the Lord's perfect timing and her house would sell in accordance with the Lord's perfect plan for her life. While I was very concerned that I would offend her, I was more concerned about being faithful to the Lord.

What an individual is saying is not nearly as important as whom they are relying on for what is being said. If we are relying on our own ability, if we are speaking from our own understanding and interpretation, we are going to be giving the best of what we have. If we are relying on the ability of the Lord, we are going to be giving the best of what the Lord determines needs to flow through us at that moment. The Lord does not always give us what we are asking for; He will oftentimes hold a word, developing our dependence and faithfulness muscles. Man on the other hand may operate from a natural love, and speak to a situation prematurely. It may be the Lord's heart for the person and it may be grounded in Scripture, but it may be out of His timing and not in the best interest of the individual to hear at that time. The gift is in operation, but the Lord is not being consulted concerning the timing. Only when our God-given ability has been returned to Him can we be confident we are allowing Him to serve His children through us. Otherwise, we are possibly taking what He has given us and operating according to our own understanding. This can cause much damage in the lives of others.

Jesus loves His church; He calls us His bride. A bride is adored, loved, and cherished. A bridegroom is very protective of the one he plans to join for eternity. The Lord has chosen to give us the delegated power and authority to be His ambassadors on this earth. An ambassador carries the heart of the one they serve. They do not make decisions or determinations as to what they think should be done. They do what they know the one they work for would do. They carry the heart of the one they serve. We are to be vessels of His heart.

He did not come to sanction our heart, our plans, and our understanding. He came to pave the way for us to die to our natural ways so we could be vessels of His heart, His plans, His understanding, and His ways. We must get out of His way and it is then that He is able to flow through us. Whatever ability you were born with, place it on the altar of God and take no ownership of His ministry through you. When our flesh is involved, it stinks to a holy God. He does not come to make our plans work; He comes to bring His plan to fruition. Our yielding to His ways allows us to be a part of that plan.

We have to give Him everything. The level to which we are able to surrender our abilities to the Lord is the level to which He can use us for His glory. He really does use the base to confound the wise. I remember hearing Phil Driscoll, the great trumpet player, testifying how he thought the Lord would require he lay down his trumpet when he was born again. To his surprise the Lord began to encourage him to play his horn. I believe there have been very few human beings that could play the trumpet like Phil Driscoll. To have that level of talent and to be entrusted by the Lord to represent Him in that gift tells me Phil Driscoll knows whose breath is flowing through his vessel. I am not technically trained in music. I just know what sounds good, but my husband has a background in music and a familiarity of instruments and an ear for the notes they play. He once commented after hearing Phil play, "He does things with his horns that technically very few people on Earth can do." He is an awesome talent and an outstanding musical technician, but there is one better. His name is Jesus. He knows how to blow the trumpet in Zion, and I believe He is the master musician through the vessel of Phil Driscoll. Would Phil have been able to develop his talent to the level it is now had he not given this ability to the Lord? Very possibly so, because the gifts and the calling are without repentance, however the music flowing through the horn would not have carried the life it now carries. He would have been gifted and called, but he would not have been chosen. There is music that touches the soul, and there is music that touches the spirit. The music flowing through that horn touches the spirit, bringing the life-giving, yoke-breaking, and life-sustaining presence of the God of Israel. I do not personally know Phil Driscoll, but I believe the Lord is giving honor where honor is due. We give God all the glory.

Several years ago it was recommended to me that I watch a documentary called *The Real Horse Whisperer*. This documentary is about Monte Roberts, who is well known for his unique style of horse training, and shows him actually training a mustang in the wild. He uses a method of trust building through pursuit that ultimately results in the horse voluntarily submitting to his training. Keeping a distance that is non-threatening and yet forever present, Mr. Roberts pursues the wild mustang, allowing him to run as far and in whatever direction he may choose. When the horse stops to rest, Mr. Roberts stops and waits. When the horse begins to run again, Mr. Roberts again pursues at a safe distance. With the constant reminder of his presence the horse begins to realize the man means no harm and eventually submits and allows him to first touch him, then saddle him, and eventually mount him and ride. Never is the animal deliberately frightened, struck, harmed, or injured in any way. The pursuit is rooted in kindness, respect, and patience. I was struck by how the method Mr. Roberts used is so similar to how the Lord deals with us, pursues us, and through a relationship of ultimate trust, wins our love and loyalty. I wept as I saw the story, because I could look back over my life and see where the love of my heavenly Father had been with me. As I applied the principles of the story I realized how similar they were to my Jesus. He will not force you, and He will continue with patience to pursue you. His love is filled with such long-suffering that He will eventually win the hardest of hearts. Jesus is the real people whisperer!

No matter what you possess in the way of ability, whether it is administrative, artistic, creative, intellectual, influential, or ministerial, yield this to the Lord. Allow Him to break and train you to do what you could never do on your own, no matter how talented and gifted you may be. Ask Him to give you the vantage point of what your ability looks like compared to His ability. We are called to be bondservants. We are called to totally yield to His will, all the time having the freedom to walk our own way.

> Blessed are the poor in spirit: for theirs is the kingdom of heaven.
>
> —MATTHEW 5:3, KJV

The truth is that we are all very poor in spirit. It is realizing this that positions us to catch the wave of His Spirit.

Give up, quit running, and quit fighting. The fight is fixed, and the sooner you yield to His care and training, the sooner you can get on with the wonderful assignment of serving Him and being His ambassador. Horses are beautiful creatures. They are beautiful in the fields, untouched and untrained. They can run with grace, beauty, strength, and power that will touch your soul. I've never seen a horse in the show ring or on the track without a harness and saddle. When that Kentucky Derby winner crosses the line, they are well aware of their feat. With nostrils flaring, sweat lathering, and eyes bulging, they take a victory lap. They always carry a jockey, and that day was always preceded by days, weeks, months, and years of hard and grueling workouts. Thoroughbreds run because they love to run, but they win races because they are trained and submitted to their rider.

Carryover Thoughts

- Your abilities are but a shadow, an indicator, of what you are called to be.
- We are to lay our abilities on the altar of God.
- The Lord does not want us to use our perfected ability; He wants us to operate in His ability.

CHAPTER 9

THE STUMBLING BLOCK OF FALSE UNITY

> Anyone who does God's will is my brother and sister and mother.
>
> —MARK 3:35

OVER THE PAST several years much emphasis has been given to the subject of unity. Church congregations have merged, pastors have formed prayer circles, and congregations of believers have become more open to the introduction of worship styles different from their own. These events in the church indicate a heart open to working together and a desire for the unity of the faith to come. It is important; however, we understand how the Lord defines this power referred to as unity. Much misconception continues to prevail in this area, giving a false sense of unity or blinding us from the true unity we now have. The act of coming together can be as much a sign of compromise as it is unity. Outward appearances cannot be the only testing ground for a unified body of Christ. Unity is of the heart. It may result in people coming together or not, and this is determined by the assignment mandated by the Lord of the church, Jesus. We are not here to build His church; we are here to serve Him and one another, and as we serve in our assigned capacity, He will build His church.

The fivefold ministry offices are set in the church for the purpose of equipping the saints for the work of the ministry until all come into the unity of the faith. The mandate on those assigned to a ministry-equipping office is to mature the body of Christ, equipping them to do the work of the ministry. This mandate to train and prepare the saints must be accomplished before saints can be expected to come into the unity of the faith. Unity must first come to the established leadership of the church. Those persons chosen by Jesus to stand in a ministry-equipping office are in unity with Him when they are in their assigned position, performing their assigned task. As they are in unity with the Lord, they will be in unity with each other. How complex we have made such a simple and well-structured plan. A football team cannot play together as a team with unity of purpose until the players of the team first know the rules of play, have been trained to execute the fundamental skills required, and have been given a position of play. So it is with the saints that they must first be equipped to perform the works of ministry before being expected to perform in the unity of the faith. To the degree this is accomplished is the degree to which unity can be accomplished.

The complexion of this unity may be much different than what we have been seeking. It will not necessarily involve all of us knowing each other and beginning to do what the other one does. It will not necessarily result in our understanding of what all members of the body of Christ are doing. It will, however, most assuredly include our respecting one another, submitting to one another in love, and accomplishing the purposes of the Father in spite of our differences. We must break the mind-set that we have to be friends and understand each other before we are in unity. These attributes are helpful, but they are not necessary. The kind of love that brings unity of purpose, unity of commitment, and unity of accomplishment has very little to do with feelings, understanding, and enjoyment.

Let us ponder this concept of friendship and what it really means to be and to have a friend. Let's look at two types of relationships that often get confused. They are buddies and friends. The two are very different, and if confused, will result in our missing what the Lord is bringing into our life through people. It is great to have buddies and enjoy their company in a social situation. It is fun to share a hobby or special interest with someone. These are life experiences. They provide "soul food," and like desserts, a little is not harmful. I believe the Lord is pleased as He watches us enjoy one another. It is wonderful when we are given people in our lives that share our opinions and interests and with whom arguments are rare. Through these relationships we are encouraged and our personalities find free expression without challenge. In our buddy relationships we are stroked, but not challenged; nurtured, but not provoked. We enjoy them, we celebrate them, and they are fun. The relationship is not deep enough for their rough edges to hit ours. Buddies know you by the flesh.

One of the biggest mistakes you will make in the area of relationships is misinterpreting your buddies as your friends and misinterpreting your friends as your enemies. Your buddies will always stand on your side; your friends will stand on the side of truth. Your buddies like you *because*; your friends love you *even though*. Your buddies know all the things about you they enjoy. Your friends know your strengths and weaknesses and love you anyway, choosing to accept your weaknesses while drawing on your strengths. Your friends love you enough to tell you the truth. Your buddies will skirt issues to avoid controversy. Thank God for buddies; they give us rest.

Friends know you by the spirit. They know you on a deeper level; your connection with them will cause your rough edges to bump against theirs. If you can walk in covenant love, you will be able to reap the benefits of this wonderful, God-given relationship. If you cannot walk in covenant love, the relationship will only be able to go so far and may be terminated all together. Friends stroke *and* challenge; nurture *and* provoke. They will stretch you and push you to the limit. You keep them in your life, not because you celebrate them all of the time, but because you tolerate them much of the time. You tolerate them because you value them, in spite of the challenges they may bring your way. I decided long ago it is better to have a friend who tolerates me than a buddy who celebrates me. The friend is in covenant, because they value me enough to put up with me. The buddy is in my life, because I bring them pleasure and do not cause them grief. I have also found that buddies are not usually around when you need a real friend. Their absence in your time of need is not always of their own choosing, but because they are not allowed there by God. They are not His choice for you in your time of need. You do not *have* to be a friend to someone; you *get* to be a friend to someone. You have the choice to say no and walk away, but the choice to say yes is a gift from God. A friend will stick closer than a brother. You may not see them often. You may not particularly enjoy doing buddy things with them, but in crucial times when you need them, somehow they are always there carrying truth for your need. The truth they carry is the Father's heart for the situation. They are allowed to have it, because they are God's friends. He is your friend, and He allows them to carry from Him what you need.

If you will allow the Lord to make this adjustment in your understanding of friendship, it will open your eyes to why certain people have been placed in your life, who they are, and why they are there. The Lord plants people of His choice in our lives for His purposes. They are either there to help us, to be helped by us, or both. We must rightly discern their purpose. The enemy also plants people in our lives for the purpose of sidetracking us. These people do not come wearing a big sign that says, "I am sent by the devil to mess you up!" They will be packaged as appealing as the enemy can package them to mess you up. It is so important to understand that most people do not know when they are being used in this way.

They are usually walking according to their own understanding and are very sincere in what they are doing. They are sincerely deceived. We must discern the sent ones and respect the decision of the Lord. He truly is the Master Personnel Manager, and He truly does know what He is doing. Unity comes when we are in obedience to His plan. Do not allow a misunderstanding of the concept of friendship and unity to separate you from the ones destined to be a part of your assignment. They need you and you need them. True unity is achieved by being connected with the right people so you may be where you are supposed to be, doing what you are supposed to do. Your flesh leaving will make room for them to stay.

Friends are friends of God, and therefore through them He can be your friend. We must realize the clashes occurring within our personalities are often not an indication of disunity, but rather an indication that carnality still exists. We can rest knowing that carnality will always exist as long as we are in this age on the earth. The best way to cope is to give it very little attention and purpose in your heart, that the mission is more important than the comfort we desire. Ironically, the comfort greatly increases once we have laid down the need to always have things our way. We must come to the understanding we are all different and unique individuals. We will never agree on everything, and yet in the midst of our human frailties, the Lord can accomplish great things through us if we are willing to yield to His lordship. The balance between fearing the Lord, walking in covenant love, and properly submitting to authority will ensure the church that Jesus Christ is in unity.

Let us examine how this may work. Since having friends and having buddies has very little to do with unity, then what is to be our focus? Our focus must become His plan, our position, and obedience to His commands. Within the confines of this focus, He will provide us with the friends and buddies we need if He feels we need them. We have to be content with what He chooses to give us. This and only this brings unity. If the body of Christ is in unity with Him, we will automatically be in unity with one another. A very good picture of the power of unity is the way the Lord has constructed the human body. Paul often used the word picture of the human body as he described the church. (See 1 Cor. 12:12–21; Rom. 12:3–5.)

I think this picture can bring great clarity to how our Lord Jesus wants His body to function.

If our body parts are working in harmony, we are able to function in health as we are designed. The same will be true of the body of Christ. If we are all in our place performing our assignment, the body of Christ will then function as it is designed. Every move of our human body is done on either a voluntary or involuntary basis. This means we have to consciously send the message to the body part to perform certain functions, while other functions are performed without conscious effort. We do not have to concentrate for our bodies to digest food. This is something done on an involuntary basis. We do not have to remember to breathe; our body will carry this out on its own. If we desire to stand up and walk, this is a conscious decision, requiring conscious effort. The incredible volume of activity occurring within the human body in one second is unfathomable. All parts must be performing their function, and the master brain coordinates these functions, thus allowing us to do the tasks desired. Cooperation on the part of all body parts is absolutely necessary. The absence of one link can bring on a chain of events that is life threatening. Ask someone who has had their heart skip just one beat. Just one beat can put you between life and death. The human body functions in unity when all parts are in proper position, performing their function. Communication does take place between the cells, but in many instances only through the brain. I pray you have ears to hear.

I would like to take one example of a natural body function to demonstrate the power and effectiveness of true unity. Let us look at the function of the colon. I purposely chose the colon because of all the body functions; it is the least appreciated when it is doing its best work. It is the responsibility of the colon to separate the toxic wastes of the body from the nutrients, transferring the nutrients back into the blood stream, and passing on the waste. When the colon is not functioning properly, many toxins are allowed to remain in the body, making it weak and polluted, and many of the nutrients designed to be transferred to the blood stream at the colon level are allowed to pass through, leaving the body undernourished. The function of the colon is not a pretty thing, but the body sure is a pretty thing when the colon is working properly.

There are persons in the body of Christ assigned to function like a colon. The product they are to focus on has been broken down, extracted from, and is in a most unpleasant form. Because of their assignment, the Lord has given them eyes to see the nutrients mixed with what needs to be removed. They are able to separate the toxic part from the beneficial part, discreetly remove the toxins, and filter back into the body the beneficial parts. Because of their love for the Lord and their love for the person and the whole body of Christ, they will not tolerate mixture. The beneficial part is presented to the body; the undesirable parts are continually separated and disposed of discreetly. It is not a glorious job to the natural eye, but so necessary. We would be well advised to appreciate the colon function of the church, because when it is not functioning properly, the whole body is polluted with toxins. We do not need to understand the function of the colon to be in unity with the colon. We need to respect and appreciate its uniqueness and value, leave it alone, and allow it to do its job.

Persons called to perform this task are usually hidden by the Lord; their assignments are covert in nature. You will know them only by the spirit as you discern their love for the Lord and for His people. They are usually found where it stinks, and if you are walking in natural understanding and not the discernment of the Lord, you will judge them as always being at the center of controversy. They are peacemakers, not peace lovers. There is a big difference! Peacemakers will start a war to bring peace. Peace lovers will compromise to maintain peace. Peacemakers bring true peace and unity; peace lovers give an appearance of peace, where disunity is at the heart and unity is espoused from the lips. There is no power, for there is no agreement.

Unfortunately there are many self-appointed colons. You will know they are not God-appointed because they do not have the love of the Father for His children. Their attacks are damaging and divisive. They believe themselves to be the watchdogs of the church, but what they actually do is expose for all to see what they believe to be error, pushing it back into the church under the mandate to expose error. This is a very polluting function to the body, and if our natural colons functioned in a similar manner for only twenty-four hours, the condition would be life threatening. The colons appointed by God might at times be visible, and they may appear to be divisive, but at the heart of their mission is the love of God and the redemptive nature of His heart. We need to flush the waste and expose the good. Knowledge of the good will teach people how to flush their own error. There are many steps we are to go through before publicly exposing error in God's children; we are all His children. Any individual's cancer can be immediately arrested by shooting them in the heart. This is a ridiculous thought to entertain, and yet we see it happen within the body we refer to as the body of Christ. Oh, how it must grieve His heart.

When I am in my place performing my assigned task, and you are in your place performing yours, we are in unity. We may not know each other this side of heaven, we may know each other and not particularly enjoy each others company, but if we are doing what we are supposed to be doing, we are in unity. Unity is not always agreeing. It is not always liking one another. It is loving the Lord enough to do our job, being quiet about what others are doing, keeping our nose in our own business, and focusing on that which the Lord is asking us to focus.

If you truly seek the Lord because you see someone performing a function you do not understand, He will give you understanding or He will tell you that you do not need to know. Either way you will be able to rest in the knowledge that He is the Lord of the church. It is not necessary for the colon to visit the heart and give it a hug. The colon just needs to extract the redemptive, put it back in the system, and discreetly remove the bad for no one else to see. That is really all the heart needs from the colon. (Just a simple reminder, all of us, unaware, have had God's servants cross our path, observe error, make the correction, and go on their way, never mentioning to us their mission. We never knew what was there and what was removed. They have been in our lives, they are in our lives, and they will continue to be sent in our lives. As the good seed of truth is planted, it will grow and choke out the bad. Not always, but most of the time, weeds can be removed in this manner. This is a beautiful picture of unity.)

False unity would have us believe we must always be in agreement on everything to be in unity. There are certain things that just don't matter. We will never agree on everything. But what we can agree on is that we love the Lord, we want the same outcome, and we will submit to the Lord and be faithful in our task. That is the agreement that brings unity. False unity perverts the concept of teamwork and loyalty, producing an emotional dishonesty that blinds the hearts of God's people. It places the focus more on behavior and less on the heart. Unity is of the heart. When it is present there is power to accomplish the task before us. When unity of the heart is absent there is no power.

There is a code of conduct in the world today called political correctness. There is nothing correct about its message, and its effects are further blinding the world to evil and influencing some segments of the church to accept compromise. This perversion is being packaged to the church in a very different form. The devil is doomed and he is defeated, but he is not stupid. Never assume you are a match for him in your own ability. Our casual approach to making major decisions without desperate dependence on the Lord is opening the door for this compromise to enter the church. It is being packaged very differently, wearing the cloak of religion. It loves to use the word *unity*.

Although the church is not as vulnerable to accept the concepts of "political correctness," I must warn that we are in danger of accepting the concepts of "spiritual correctness." This is not an invitation to go on a witch hunt exposing all the methods being used to bring error into the church. This is an invitation to get on your knees and to know your God in a way deeper than you have ever known Him. It is only by knowing Him that you will be able to discern the counterfeit. The devil has more packages for the counterfeit than your brain can imagine. There is only one real Jesus. Know Him, and there is no counterfeit that will be able to deceive you. You are no match for the deceiver in your own strength. The deceiver is no match for your Jesus. Hug His garment!

One of the ways spiritual correctness is being cloaked and presented to the church is in the false concept of unity, a concept telling us we must not offend others. We must all get along. It is one thing to get along by forbearing one another and quite another by compromising. Forbearance is a fruit of the spirit; compromise is a fruit of evil. Unfortunately the truth offends. This is not an invitation to be unkind, for truth must always be balanced with mercy. If you are carrying the Father's heart, this balance will be present. However, even when you are carrying truth in the perfect balance with mercy, it will offend someone not wanting to hear the truth. No matter how you package truth to wrap it with mercy, if you have not compromised the truth, the sparks will fly when it hits darkness. You will never be able to deliver truth in a dark place and not have a reaction from the darkness.

Jesus said He did not come into this world to bring peace but division. (See Matt. 10:34.) He came to the world to bring division between light and darkness. He came to the church to bring unity in the spirit. If we are doing the work of the Lord and are operating in a worldly principle, we are representing the world, and therefore are against Him. He will come and bring truth exposing the darkness. He is not against us; He is against our methods. He is drawing a line so we may step into the light so we may be perfect as our Father in heaven is perfect. His purposes are always redemptive. If we are separated from Him, it is by our choice, not His. Only when we are doing the work of the Lord and operating in obedience to His ways are we in unity with Him. It doesn't matter how well we are getting along with others. If we are not in unity with Jesus we are not operating in the spirit of unity.

There is also a false concept of common purpose. We cannot all have the same fervor for the same focus. What the Lord has assigned one group of people to focus on may be very different than my focus. They are not called to be involved with my focus any more than I am called to be involved in theirs. I am not against them, because I do not get involved with their ministry. I am against them when I am not doing my assignment, because no matter how unrelated it may appear to the natural eye, if I am not in my place doing my assignment, it will adversely affect them. The Lord is the Commander in Chief of His armed forces.

The common purpose we are to focus on is Jesus. Our common purpose must be to love the Lord our God with all our hearts, and to serve Him with obedience. This is the only and most powerful purpose we must have. This does not give us free reign to do anything we want to do, anytime we want to do it. There are laws of submission and authority that draw the boundaries to prevent insubordination and defiance. These boundaries, balanced with an unyielding commitment to truth, will keep us out of trouble.

It is wonderful when congregations of different forms of worship can come together for the common purpose of serving. This surely must touch the Father's heart to see His children come together. If by our coming together we must compromise the truths we have come to know by His Word, the power we have come to experience, we have compromised the truth. Relationships may be formed, there may be a form of godliness, but the power of the gospel has been denied. We must come together in spite of our differences, in forbearance of one another, for the common purpose of loving and serving Him.

There is a dividing line where the servant of the Lord must stand on the side of truth. When you do, you will be divided from the compromise; you will not be in compliance with the standards of spiritual correctness.

When you must compromise truth for the purpose of not offending, in order to bring unity, you have fallen prey to a false unity designed by the devil to choke the power of the gospel!

This is what false unity is designed to accomplish. It is designed to choke the power of the gospel. Another way of saying this is that it is designed to pervert the plan of God and silence the voice of God. The one who comes to do this is the enemy of our soul. Always know that where there is a plan of God, there is a perverted counterfeit offered in a religions form. This is what the enemy does through a perverted form of religion to bring about a system that is anti-Christ. Do not try to save your own life, for that is when you will lose it. Stand always in the place of truth, absent of fear and intimidation, knowing Jesus is a shield about you and the lifter of your head. (See Ps. 3:3.) Be in perfect unity with your Father. He will insure, by the love shed abroad in your heart, that you are in the true unity that pleases Him.

Carryover Thought

- Unity occurs when each member of the body is in their assigned position, doing what they have been instructed to do. (See 1 Cor. 12:18.)

CHAPTER 10

THE SAFETY NET OF AUTHORITY AND SUBMISSION

Obey your spiritual leaders and do what they say. Their work is to watch over your souls, and they know they are accountable to God. Give them reason to do this joyfully and not with sorrow. That would certainly not be for your benefit.

—HEBREWS 13:17

And now, a word to you who are elders in the churches. I, too, am an elder and a witness to the sufferings of Christ. And I, too, will share his glory and his honor when he returns. As a fellow elder, this is my appeal to you: Care for the flock of God entrusted to you. Watch over it willingly, not grudgingly—not for what you will get out of it, but because you are eager to serve God. Don't lord it over the people assigned to your care, but lead them by your good example. And when the head Shepherd comes, your reward will be a never-ending share in his glory and honor. You younger men, accept the authority of the elders. And all of you, serve each other in humility, for "God sets himself against the proud, but he shows favor to the humble." So humble yourselves under the mighty power of God, and in his good time he will honor you. Give all your worries and cares to God, for he cares about what happens to you. Be careful! Watch out for attacks from the Devil, your great enemy. He prowls around like a roaring lion, looking for some victim to devour. Take a firm stand against him, and be strong in your faith. Remember that your Christian brothers and sisters all over the world are going through the

> same kind of suffering you are. In his kindness God called you to his eternal glory by means of Jesus Christ. After you have suffered a little while, he will restore, support, and strengthen you, and he will place you on a firm foundation. All power is his forever and ever. Amen.
>
> —1 Peter 5:1–11

Through the information contained in this writing, it is my sincere desire to see God's people walk free from the chains that bind them and walk in the freedom that will allow them to walk in their destiny. Stumbling blocks thrown in our paths by the enemy have been exposed, allowing the yokes placed on the necks of God's people to be broken. The yokes bear the names of fear, fear of man, offense, works, compromise, natural knowledge, pride, and self-reliance. These are placed there by the enemy to steal the joy of our salvation and to thwart or stop altogether the plan of God for our lives. I praise God for His freedom, I praise God for His truth, and I am humbled He allowed me the privilege to pen these truths.

Broken yokes must be replaced by the Lord's yoke, which He promises is easy. (See Matt. 11:29–30.) If we do not submit to His lordship, we will use our freedom to go our own way and will be wearing the yoke of rebellion. It is of utmost importance to realize freedom comes with a balancing force called responsibility. For every freedom given there is a responsibility to handle that freedom in a godly manner.

The Lord has established a system for protecting His children and teaching them to properly and safely walk in the freedom He has granted. This is achieved by placing those of His choice in authority over us. Proper submission to authority established by the Lord will keep us in the protective hand of our heavenly Father, who loves us with a love we cannot imagine. We must understand this, we must trust this, and we must walk in obedience to the path the Lord chooses, or we will never walk in the destiny He has planned.

A picture that clearly defines the safety of properly established authority is the military force. The dividing lines of responsibility and authority are clearly defined and communicated, with each individual having a place and being expected to stay in their place performing their assignment as instructed. Every level of responsibility is given the authority needed to perform the function of the position. Every person has authority to perform their assigned task and also is under the authority of those assigned above them. To repeat, everyone has a level of authority, and everyone is under authority. When this system of organization is operating as established and good leadership and management are present, order is in operation and objectives are met.

No one enters the military as a general. They may be destined to be a general, but the fulfillment of this is achieved only through the successful completion of prescribed preparation and time. As they are faithful with entry-level responsibilities, in safe increments they will be given more responsibility and therefore increased authority. Promotion comes with proving.

Serving the Lord is very similar. As we are faithful in what is set before us, we will be given more as the Lord prescribes. We do not decide how we are to be trained. We do not decide who will be our superior officer. The Lord does this with our best interest in mind. To seek Him for His plan and to submit to His plan for our development is to submit to His lordship. Submission to His lordship is the *only way* we will be allowed to step into the destiny He has for us. The Lord desires to complete His work through us, but without our willingness to endure the training He prescribes and submit to the timing He ordains, this will not be accomplished no matter how much we want it and no matter how much the Lord wants it for us. He honors His Word, and His decisions are just and true. He cannot compromise His ways. His mercy is what holds us back when we have not allowed Him to prepare us for what it is we think we are to do.

Gifts deposited in us are present from the beginning of our existence. There are times they are dormant, and there are times they are apparent. We are given glimpses of what the Lord has deposited in others and us. We must accurately discern and wait on His timing and leading for releasing us into the operation of the gifts. We are *called* from the foundation of this world. We are *chosen* when we have allowed the Lord to do the necessary work and development in us to insure we do not damage ourselves and others. This is not to say we will never make a mistake, hurt someone, or be in error. These are inevitable human experiences, and we would be foolish to think we are above any of them. However, when a servant of the Lord has waited on the timing of the Lord for promotion and position, mistakes will be quickly discerned and corrected. If we have allowed the Lord to establish the channels of communication He desires, if we are sensitive to His heart, He can quickly get our attention when we have allowed ourselves to deviate from His ways. Operating in a God-given gift earlier than the Lord releases may result in error and damage to others and ourselves. Before the Lord will release you to your next level of responsibility, it will be necessary that your character be able to support the assignment.

It is for this reason the Lord will map a course of "learning experiences" to include specific people and places. This course is designed to build our spiritual house and equip us for the assignment He has for us. Our first assignment will be to know Him. It is imperative that we know the Lord before attempting to work for Him. To be an ambassador for Christ we must know Him, as we will not be representing ourselves but will be representing Him. It will be this knowing Him that will lay the foundation for all He will be and do in and through us.

It must be the timing of the Lord as we advance in the different levels of servanthood. Just as the picture we are using for clarification, a soldier has no direct authority to promote himself. The power the soldier is given is to perform the assigned task to the best of his ability, being faithful in what he has been given to do. The first assignment we have is to know the Lord. Worship Him, learn of Him, spend time with Him, and you will grow in your love and knowledge of Him.

Once we have established a foundation of knowing the real, the Lord will begin to advance us through a series of preparatory experiences. These experiences will be designed to continue to bring us into a deeper fellowship and knowledge of Him, as well as train us for our assignment. I can remember advancing through my college curriculum, fulfilling the requirements for a diploma. There were certain basic courses all students were required to have, regardless of their major course of study. I can remember delaying a freshman level class simply because I had no desire to take the course, and furthermore it had nothing to do with the subject matter of the specific degree I was seeking. The fact remained that it was a requirement for the degree, and so as a senior I had to take a freshman level course in summer school before being allowed to graduate.

This is very similar to the way of the Lord. In His wisdom there are courses required that simply must be taken in order to advance in servanthood. You will never be allowed to skirt around these requirements. Some possible examples are: Housekeeping 101, Childcare 205, Sit in Your Seat and Be Quiet 303, and Love the Unlovable 402. These are a sampling of some of the required undergraduate courses, and if you are obedient, they will provide unbelievable opportunities for learning and development. You never outgrow the requirement for refresher courses in these areas.

Graduate courses will have names like Submitting to Authority Even When it Is Harsh 535, Following the Holy Ghost Even When You Think You Have a Better Idea 555, and Submitting to the Law of Love and Forgiveness As You Pull the Spear From Your Side 656. If we are not able to submit to the lordship of Jesus and successfully complete these courses, we will never be able to overcome an enemy purposed to destroy our destiny and the destiny of those we are destined to touch. It does not matter how gifted we are. If we have not submitted to the lordship of Jesus and successfully completed the required courses, we will never fulfill the destiny He has for us. We will be used of Him to some degree, but we will not be all He has called us to be unless we complete the requirements. This will insure we will not be harmed or harm others. The Lord will not place a bazooka in the hands of a baby. If a spiritual baby is operating in power without wisdom, it has not been ordained of the Lord. It has been taken without permission. The Lord releases us to operate in the gifting He has given as we submit to His lordship and to those He places above us. The power to overcome circumstances comes by submitting to the Lord, and we learn this by submitting to His servants.

The servants of the Lord are not chosen because they are perfect. There is no one on the earth perfect. There will be times we are asked by God to endure what may seem to be harshness, unfairness, and misunderstanding. This may or may not be the case. There are times we feel someone is being harsh and unfair. We may feel totally misunderstood. It is very possible we may be too naive to properly understand. As a teenager I constantly judged my parents to be harsh, unfair, and not understanding of my point of view. I shudder to think what would have happened to me had I been allowed to go my own way. They were good parents, and their restrictions were a safety net for me. This is not to infer they were always in the right. I am certain there were times my assessments were correct, but that would never have justified defiance and disobedience.

Likewise the Lord will place leadership in your path that will sometimes seem to be harsh, unfair, and not understanding of you.

Sometimes it will seem this way, and sometimes it will actually be this way. Rest in the knowledge that if the authority has been ordained of the Lord, He will use even the harsh and unfair things to develop you. We are to submit to the authority placed over us, even when it is harsh, knowing all the while we are pleasing the Lord as we endure the hardship.

I hear some hearts in panic. Let me interject a bit of damage control. We are not to submit to abuse, and if you have been or believe you are now a recipient of abuse, rest in the knowledge that God hates it and does not expect you to remain in an abusive situation. Later in the chapter we will be developing guidelines for knowing the difference between harshness and abuse, so stay with me here because a person who has been abused (spiritually, emotionally, or physically) may wrongly interpret godly authority as abusive because of the unhealed wounds of the past. There is healing available and even though it may seem unfair, it is still necessary for you to learn to trust again and to properly submit to God-ordained authority.

We are to honor our fathers and our mothers in the natural and the same is true with our heavenly Father and those that He ordains to watch over us. They hold keys for our life we will obtain no other way. The Lord places the keys there for us. Yes, they are ours, and yes, they are from the Lord, but He chooses to pass them through those ordained to be our spiritual fathers and mothers. If we do not submit to their authority, we will not receive from them what the Lord has ordained for us to receive. We must trust the Lord, knowing He will do His part; our job is to do ours. Those in authority over us must hold a place of honor if for no other reason than God placed them there. We are to love them, respect them, and give them honor by submitting to their authority.

It is important to realize we do not always pick our leader. This, like the military, is often decided for us. Left to our own choice, we would pick those we tend to enjoy being around or appear to have the framework we need for advancement. So many mistakes are made when this is done, because the primary motivation is comfort and ambition. This will never result in advancement of any value. Conversely, we may avoid those who hit our rough edges. This is the part of development we must be willing to endure, because our rough edges must be smooth before we can step into our next assignment. We will be given leaders we enjoy and those we have to work at enjoying. Whatever the case, they have what we need; we are there by divine assignment. Obedience is our only requirement.

The question sometimes arises, how do I know who I am assigned to? Begin with where you are. Submit to the authority now in place over your life, and the Lord will lead you as you walk in submission. If you have ever left a fellowship out of offense, not allowing the Lord to give you grace for the situation, or waiting on His timing for leaving, repent for your self-will and ask the Lord what He is requiring of you in the situation. Discuss this with your pastor or those leaders presently in your life. You cannot change the past, but you can from this day forward, submit to the lordship of Jesus, refusing to map your own steps another day.

There are three primary functions we are to fill within the ministry fellowship we are assigned. Each of these will require submission to authority. We are first there to receive training, development, healing, and correction. We are there to be discipled. Secondly, we are there to be a blessing naturally. In most instances we should be involved in the ministry of helps. And third, at some point there should be an outlet for the flow of ministry coming from us to others. We will not necessarily operate in all three of these functions at one time.

We should always be operating in the first function of receiving. The Lord has a unique way of providing for the development of all concerned. A submissive and obedient heart will go a long way in setting you up for receiving all He has for you. Even a dry message can minister life if your heart is open to receive. Your expectation has a great deal to do with what comes through the vessel of the Lord to you.

I do not believe it is accurate to assume everyone is to always be involved in the ministry of helps. As a general rule, we all need to pull our weight, helping in the natural functions required to keep the operation of the ministry going. An exception to this is the person instructed of the Lord to take some bench time or the one hiding behind busyness. If you believe the Lord is instructing you in this manner and you feel very uncomfortable sitting and just receiving for a short season, you are probably a very good candidate for this sabbatical. It is not to be forever, but there are times it is very ordained. Submit to this leading, and soon you will be strong and more able to help others.

The third function comes as you grow in your knowledge of Him. Life is being imparted to all of us, life that will eventually begin to overflow from us. We minister from our overflow. We minister from our relationship with the Lord and our intimate time spent with Him. As this occurs there is a well springing up from within that is hard to contain. Your local fellowship should have an outlet for you. It may not be the outlet you desire, but if you will submit to whatever you are offered, the Lord will bless you in ways only experience can reveal. Be a light where you are.

Ministry leadership opportunities are given as the Lord chooses. Not everyone is called to serve in a ministry-equipping office. However, we are all called to do the work of the ministry as we are trained. Those assigned to a ministry-equipping function are appointed by Jesus to teach and train the body of Christ to do the work of the ministry. They are much like the professors of an institution of higher learning. Much of the time, in addition to doing, they are teaching others to do. If you have been called by God to a ministry-equipping office, then you will be promoted in His perfect timing. You have to rest, submitting to His timing and to the authority placed over you. Continue to walk with the Lord. As you know Him and learn of Him your destiny will be fulfilled. He promises! (See Gal. 1:15–17.)

To be given a leadership position requires the Lord to promote and the leader to appoint the position. You may feel you are ready to step into a position of authority and leadership. You may be right; you may be wrong. The truth is if you have not been offered a position, you are to submit to that decision by your leader, like it or not. The very act of not accepting the decision is all that is needed to disqualify you for the position. Do not fail this test of submission. This is God's required course for graduation. You have to take it and you have to pass it, or you will not be advanced. There is only one gate at this stage of development, and it is narrow. There is no way around it. There is no way over it. There is no way under it. You must go through it!

Purpose in your heart to stand faithful, determined to wait on God's timing. He is more than able to advance you when He says the time is now. It is better to be a mouse in front of a freight train at full speed than a human vessel standing in the way of an almighty God when He is ready to move. Rest knowing that when it is your time, God will touch the heart of those linked to your destiny. He will see to it you are advanced in His perfect timing. You may think you are ready, but the fact you have not been advanced indicates you are not. Submit to this: rest in the knowledge that He is in control. Just trust Him!

Even if you believe with no doubt that your leader is not placing you where you think you should be placed, and let's assume for the sake of this lesson you are correct, it is still out of order for you to take matters into your own hands and operate in defiance or seek another leader. The Lord places leaders in the body and He gives them responsibility and authority necessary for the assignment. In keeping with His ways, the Lord is not going to operate the leader as a puppet on a string. That is not how He works. When a leader makes a mistake, the Lord does not automatically intervene, making things the way we think they should be or even the way He thinks they should be. He will respect the decision of the leader. You are expected to do the same. (Hint: It is a test. Do not take matters into you own hands or you will have to take the test again!)

Certainly the Lord does not forever allow gross error and will intervene eventually as He deems necessary, but there are many mistakes the Lord overlooks from His leaders. We are well advised to submit, laying it at the Lord's feet for handling. You may not always understand, but you can always rest knowing that you will be given everything He has for you when He wants to give it to you—not a minute sooner; not a minute later. The quickest way for you to delay your advancement is to take the reigns in your hands and promote yourself. You will hate your position. It will bring you nothing but sorrow, and it will hurt the heart of the Father who loves you so much and wants to see you succeed. The only person capable of altering His will for you is *you*!

As we walk this walk of submission there will be times our hearts will cry to the Lord for clarity and guidance. The farther we advance down this road of preparation, the narrower the path becomes. The left margin is labeled "Submitting to and pleasing my God-ordained authority" and the right "Submitting to and pleasing my Jesus." These two margins should never be in opposition, and yet there will be times you will think you cannot do both at the same time. Let us seek the Lord for guidance.

One of the first cries for understanding coming from the heart of a servant wanting to be in proper submission will be the cry to understand where appropriate disagreement ends and insubordination begins. There will always be occasions where you do not agree with decisions made. This may be because you do not have all the facts. It may be because you have not walked long enough with the Lord to have understanding, or it may be you have a very good point. To properly handle these situations will go a long way to insuring you stay out of trouble with the Lord and are also a blessing to your leader and the body.

You must always remember it is the leader who will stand before the Lord accountable for the decisions made with regard to those entrusted to His care. In those times when you are in disagreement there should always be the freedom to respectfully and honestly express what is in your heart. If, however, after you have done this, the leadership determines to proceed anyway, you must acquiesce resting in the knowledge you are not the one placed by the Lord in the position of leadership. This guideline applies to all situations except decisions in direct opposition to the laws of God or the laws of the land. Certainly we are to never commit sin or break legal laws at the command of leadership. Decisions we do not understand or decisions seeming unfair or unwise that do not require the breaking of laws are to be handled between the Lord and His leaders. Again, there should always be freedom for sincere questions and expression of disagreement done with respect and order. If the information is not received we need to respect the decision and rest in the knowledge that we are not the one responsible.

Submission is a heart condition. It is not acceptable to speak words of agreement all the while determined to resist in your heart. Psychologists call this *passive-aggression*. God calls it *rebellion*. Submission of the heart does not require the attitude that says, "You are right. I agree." Submission may say, "You may be wrong; I may be wrong; but you're the boss, and I'm going to do my best to help." If you can approach situations with this attitude you will learn a great deal and stay in proper submission to the leadership placed above you by the Lord. Your leader's job is to seek the Lord and lead accordingly. Your job is to get under the covering and follow. It is your place of safety. If you will respect the position of the leader, you will eventually get to where you are supposed to be, and the Lord will be pleased with your submission.

Insubordination is not when you sincerely disagree and reserve opinion. Insubordination occurs when you determine to take matters in your own hands, going against the methods requested by leadership. It is not your place or your decision, and even if you are 100 percent right, you will be 100 percent wrong. Your actions will be very displeasing to the Lord and will place you in direct opposition to Him. That is not a good place to be!

The next level to the above test graduates from disagreement and insubordination to the line where your attempt to stand in truth becomes rebellion. Same situation; more extreme circumstances. We must all be committed to truth and as we mature in our relationship with the Lord and become more intimate with Him, we will find ourselves in situations where we are a standard for truth. Raising a standard of truth will always have a high cost, because truth confronts darkness. For instance when you grow in the knowledge of the power of your words and you no longer allow yourself to be involved in conversation displeasing to the Lord, this standard will not be well received by those wanting to continue displeasing conversation in your company. This truth will confront the darkness trying to operate in your midst. It is not necessary for you to say anything. All you have to do is refuse to come into agreement and refuse to add to the conversation. This action alone will cause the sparks to fly in the spirit realm. Depending on the others involved, they will either raise their standard or detest your company.

Taking this same scenario, let's assume the ones doing the chattering are in authority over you. Real challenge. Even though you know this conversation is displeasing to the Lord and you refuse to participate, it is not your place to take the matter further. You must also not lower your standard. You are responsible for your actions, not the actions of others. It is not your place to force and demand correction. Be respectful, refuse to conform, and trust the Lord to correct as He deems appropriate. Do not fear what man thinks; do not be concerned for the cost of not being "one of the boys." Fear God, He will keep you.

Error on the part of your leader does not give you the freedom to disrespect their position. You must never lower a standard, but you must never assume the position of judge either. When you are entrusted by the Lord to see a weakness in your leader, do not take this as justification to not respect them, but rather continue to submit to their authority. Otherwise, you will be in rebellion. We are to stand for truth, not push truth. We are to be witnesses.

God's appointed leaders are to be given respect, not because they are deserving and not because they are always right, but because of where they have been placed by the Lord. Period! There are no *but*s that apply in this situation. Respect them when they are wonderful; respect them when they are difficult. You don't have to like them; you don't have to agree with them; you don't have to feel all warm and fuzzy inside; you simply need to be respectful of their position. Feelings have very little to do with respect.

Again, the life of King David gives us such a perfect example of this principle. Certainly he refused to raise his hand to King Saul, even when Saul was clearly in error. This story is so full of pictures to illustrate the proper position we are to take when we are being harshly treated. However, let's look at another chapter in the life of David that I believe gives a clear picture of absolute rebellion against God-ordained authority. Let's examine the relationship David had with his son Absalom and how it applies to the principle being taught.

You can read the story in 2 Samuel 13. David's son Amnon committed the unthinkable betrayal against his sister Tamar, a sister Absalom loved dearly. Amnon lusted for his sister, tricked her to coming to his bed, and in the face of her trust and love for him raped her, stripping Tamar of something she could never again regain. As if this were not enough, Amnon then cruelly rejected Tamar, hating her as much as he had lusted for her, causing her to be shamed before all of Israel. Absalom loved his sister and was outraged by the injustice his brother had done. There was a cry from the heart of Absalom for justice and it was his father, David, who would decide the punishment. To Absalom's great sorrow his father and king did not punish Amnon as severely as would seem appropriate for the crime committed.

David was not only ruling on the crime as the father of Amnon, but also as the king of the land. The punishment did not seem to fit the crime and Absalom was in strong disagreement with his father and his king. Assuming a position of authority not given him by his father or the Lord, Absalom took matters into his own hands and killed Amnon, vindicating his sister. It is so understandable why Absalom was hurt and desired vengeance. It is so understandable; it was so wrong. He disqualified himself from ever being given the authority he desired. Because he killed his brother? It certainly was not pleasing to the Lord for him to murder his brother, but that was not what disqualified him. He failed the test, because he did not accept and respect the decision of his father and his king. He tried to right a perceived wrong when he did not understand or agree with the outcome. It seemed unfair to him and he thought he had a better idea for punishment. He did not have the authority to do this, and he was in big trouble.

Absalom killed a guilty man and was rejected by God. David killed an innocent man and was still allowed to rule as king. These two historical events alone are enough to show the importance the Lord places on honoring His established authority.

This is one of the most deceptive stumbling blocks, and it will absolutely knock you from your place of authority if you fall prey to its trickery. You must honor and respect God-established authority. In His timing He will remove authority not operating in keeping with His divine plan. You have to leave these matters to Him for handling. View them as a hot potato and take them immediately to the feet of Jesus. It is forbidden fruit.

We must not touch God's anointed. What this means is that we must not step into the place of doing what we think they should do. It does not mean we always agree and approve of their actions and decisions. It simply means we see, we respectfully express our position, and we leave the matter to the Lord for handling. To assume a position not given by the Lord can bring judgment from Him. I am going to share a story from my life, as I believe it so clearly illustrates this principle and the deception surrounding the pit we may fall into without even knowing what has happened.

Within a fellowship I was attending, there existed an individual experiencing some very difficult times emotionally and financially. I was aware of the circumstances and thought many times how I might be able to help. I really did not know all the facts surrounding the situation, but it was my understanding our corporate local body was not consistently helping this person. Most assistance given came from a few isolated individuals.

One Sunday morning I decided to give this person some money as I was preparing my morning offering. There was a genuine need, and I had the ability to help in the need. It was my plan to give this as we mingled and greeted one another during the service. Surprisingly she moved forward and sat directly behind me just before the offering was taken. I thought God was confirming my plan. I turned to her, but for some reason, was unable to give the money. I concluded that the Lord wanted me to wait until after the service.

There were certain things said in the morning message that continued to cause me to hesitate concerning giving the money. The need was so real I could not understand why it would not be acceptable to help in some small way. In spite of this, I continued to feel a check in the pit of my stomach. Thankfully I have walked long enough with the Lord to suffer the consequences of running yellow lights, so I decided I would withhold action until I had a clear green light to proceed.

Immediately following the service as I was driving home, the Lord began to deal with me concerning the money and the person in need. He began to have a conversation with me concerning why I was giving the money. I truly believed it was because there was a genuine need, and I wanted to help in some way. To a degree this was absolutely true, but the Lord began to reveal to me a hidden motive of my heart. I did not like what I saw, and I hope I never have to go through that situation again.

The Lord asked me, "Why are you giving the money?" To which I responded, "Because she needs it, Lord." The Lord then asked me, "How do you feel about the fact that the pastor has not done more on behalf of the fellowship to help this individual?" BOOM! There it was. I had been nailed by the Lord! I immediately realized I had judged my pastor as being insensitive to this person's needs. I had judged the body as not being a body sensitive to the ones right in their midst, and I was taking it on myself to do what I thought the pastor and others should be doing. There are really no words to express the shudder I felt inside. There is an element of the fear of the Lord when you realize you have done something very wrong and you want very quickly to correct the situation before you have to suffer the consequences of your error. This is the way I felt that morning. We should be grateful when the Lord disciplines. It is His love that brings forth His correction. He did not want me to make this mistake.

This is the understanding the Lord gave me that day. It was not the giving of the money that bothered Him. I truly believe He desired for this person to have the assistance. I was not allowed to give the money because of my heart motive. I was about to do the right thing for a very wrong reason, all the while thinking I was doing a good deed. Human pride is so very ugly. We are to be the hands of Jesus, the legs of Jesus, and the mouthpiece of Jesus. We should strive to be the repairer of the breech, not the corrector of the wrong. The corrector operates from judgment; the repairer is operates from love. We do not *have to* help people; we *get to* help people, and on that day I was not allowed to help someone because of a *stinking heart motive.* I believe the Lord said, "Gee, Terri, I wish I could let you be my hands in this situation, but you just do not qualify today. You are wearing a coat of judgment, and that is My garment." I had judged my pastor and members of the congregation as insensitive to the needs of this family. I was out of order and very displeasing to the Lord. Was I right in my assessment? There is a good possibility I was. But rest assured, even if I was 100 percent right in my assessment, my actions were 100 percent wrong in the eyes of the Lord. Consequently I was denied the blessing of being God's extended hand to that family because of my stinking heart motive. I experienced godly sorrow, repentance, and His forgiveness. I love Him so much; I pray I never do that again!

The Lord further led me to understand that my pastor had been given the role of leader over the local body. He will stand accountable for how well he is the watch keeper over the souls of God's precious people. This particular person had submitted to the leadership of the pastor, and it was out of order for me to try and correct a perceived wrong. I did not have that authority. To try and interject the assistance I determined was appropriate was assuming a place of responsibility and authority I had not been given by the Lord. The spirit that operated through Absalom was trying to operate through me. I cannot say whether or not the Lord is pleased with the level of assistance this person was getting from the local church body, but I can tell you that it was not my place to judge, and the Lord will deal with the situation in His perfect timing. There are many things I did not know and many pieces of the puzzle I did not have. It was my place to pray and help as the Lord lead and to reserve an opinion on the situation. There is always the possibility I was very wrong in my perception.

This incident may never have been known by anyone, but I would have disqualified myself as one the Lord could trust to respect lines of authority and submission. I pray you have ears to hear.

This last cry from our heart for clarification is one we hear much about in the church as well as our secular society. The word *abuse* is thrown around in all circles. We have become very abuse conscious in this country. This focus has caused people who never considered themselves to be victims of abuse to resurrect old situations and assume the position of victim. One of the unfortunate consequences of all the increased awareness is that the very real situations, where abuse is present, become clouded in the midst of all the hyper accusation, and consequently may not receive the attention so desperately needed.

As I am concluding this chapter, it is my sincere prayer to the Lord to establish guidelines for His people relative to this area. I believe He has granted that request.

When abuse is present there is a line that is crossed where harsh and inappropriate treatment by authority becomes abuse. To know the difference is imperative, or we will continue to remove ourselves from situations that may be harsh and unfair, but are not abusive in the Lord's eyes. We must be able to discern the difference so we do not separate ourselves from those we are called to be connected with or stay in situations God is not asking us to endure. To clarify the distinction between abuse and harshness will prevent us from backing away from the very training the Lord has ordained.

Abuse is a trap laid by the enemy in an attempt to bind you in chains. Harshness is simply man's behavior that is not in keeping with God's nature that will require you to obey God's commands at the peril of your natural nature. Abuse is the enemy using another to harm the real you; it is intended to damage you emotionally and spiritually. Harshness on the other hand is the result of the fallen nature of man where an individual behaves in a way inconsistent with the Lord's way and requires you to walk in obedience to forebear and forgive. Abuse is designed to alter who you are in your spirit. Harshness will make you uncomfortable but if you respond properly it will be used of the Lord to train and develop you into who He has called you to be in your spirit. While harsh treatment is not from the Lord, it can still be used by Him. Abuse goes straight for the heart and is after your free will. Harshness, on the other hand, messes with your flesh and asks you to properly exercise your free will. Abuse is perverted spiritual contact; harshness is a lack of good people skills. Abuse is spirit powered and goes for the spirit; harshness is soul powered and goes for the soul. In light of this perspective let us look at where one ends and the other begins.

To be under the authority of a harsh and unfair leader may be a difficult challenge. It may alter the enjoyment of your journey, but in the end it will not harm you, and it will be used of the Lord to develop you. I do not believe the Lord instructs others to be harsh for our development. This is not in keeping with His ways. But I do know the Lord will take even the unfair treatment and use it for our good. There have been many great leaders who were harsh and very unreasonable yet accomplished great things for the Lord and for the world. This behavior was certainly not pleasing to the Lord. This behavior certainly needed to be corrected for the person to be the best they could be. However, the greatness of their accomplishments were made possible not because they were so wonderful, but because they were appointed by the Lord to be the leader, and recognizing this, those assigned to support them were willing to forebear their irrational, ridiculous, and inexcusable behavior for the good of all.

A world leader that immediately comes to mind is Sir Winston Churchill. What an awesome leader he was for Great Britain. His quick and dry wit, which is so British, was so much fun to savor. He touched the world with his leadership and wisdom. To this day contemporary leaders, theologians, and historians study his writings and insights. He is an absolute joy to study; and yet there were many times he was an absolute terror to serve.

When you research the working conditions of those appointed to be a part of his support staff, you discover the treatment they received may be considered abusive by today's standards. Was it abusive or just harsh? The Lord placed this great man in his position of leadership, because we know it is the Lord who raises up and puts down kings. Also assigned to serve him were those chosen to carry out the necessary support functions that allowed him to accomplish his assignment. Individuals like Hastings Ismay, Churchill's minister of defense, and Alan Brooke, chairman of the chiefs of staff committee. These were truly great men willing to sacrifice fame for the better of all.

One of Churchill's private secretaries, Elizabeth Nel, recounted the experience of taking dictation. She recalled how he would mumble while dictating correspondence, because there was usually a cigar in his mouth. His well-deserved reputation of having an explosive temper made asking him to repeat himself an option not considered. She expressed her absolute fear of not hearing what he said the first time, because she was expected to get it right the first time—no mistakes, no questions. She later said of Churchill in a memoir, "He did not mean to be unkind. He was just heart and soul engaged in winning the war." That is loyalty!

Churchill was thought to be insensitive to the personal needs of his staff, often requiring them to work long hours without breaks. This certainly sounds like harsh and unfair treatment. To regularly work in this type of environment may result in health-related complications due to the constant stress level. Yet as you listen to this woman recount her days of service, her admiration, respect, and genuine affection for this great leader is apparent. She clearly was able to look beyond the human frailties, endeavoring to forbear in her commitment to doing her part to help fulfill the mandate resting on this man's shoulders. I believe it was very pleasing to the Lord for her to submit to this man, because without the staff support of her and many others, Churchill would not have been able to accomplish his mission.

History recalls the greatness of Churchill and this memory is well deserved. In the Lord's eyes all of those who stayed in their place of assignment, did what they were told to do, and submitted to the authority placed over them even when harsh held a place of honor equal to the one so visible to the world. You may never have heard of Hastings Ismay, Alan Brooke, or Elizabeth Nel. Yet they greatly impacted all of our lives, because it was their faithful commitment and loyalty to a man known to be an absolute tyrant at times that allowed him to accomplish what he was destined to do and be for England and the world.

It is a great experience when we are able to enjoy the ones we are called to serve and to serve with. This however cannot become a requirement as there will be many times we are not allowed this luxury. The pursuit to fulfill your destiny will require you to work with people because of what the Lord has put in them, not because you will enjoy their personalities. It is not abusive for a person to be harsh. It is not abusive for a person to be difficult. It is not abusive for a person to make your flesh scream. It may be rude; it may be childish; it may be immature behavior; but it is not abusive.

It is abusive for a person in authority over you to allow the enemy to operate through them for the purpose of binding you in chains, interfering with your fellowship with the Lord, and altering your God-ordained destiny.

Harsh leadership will cause you to experience great discomfort in your soul. Your flesh will be affected, and it can actually be a good indicator of how much flesh you need to allow the Lord to crucify. It is soul motivated and affects your soul. You will deal with emotions of anger, frustration, disgust, judgment, criticism, discouragement, and the list goes on. Although these emotions may be warranted, we are required of the Lord to stay submitted, faithful, and respectful. The Lord will use these difficult times to train you, teaching you how to do a job in spite of the conditions. You will learn to focus and purpose in your heart to please the Lord no matter the cost. Here comes a very clear dividing line. When you are experiencing harsh treatment you will be driven to the Lord for comfort. The compromises you must make and the concessions you must agree to have no eternal significance and do not break His laws.

Abuse on the other hand is aimed toward your spirit. It is spiritually motivated, spiritually damaging, and spiritually discerned. Spiritual abuse may manifest in harsh and unkind treatment; it may manifest in sweet and gentle treatment. The result will always be a separation from the Lord and bondage. Just because someone is being pleasant in their approach does not necessarily indicate they are not being abusive. Conversely an extremely harsh unkind treatment may not necessarily be considered abuse. Where harsh treatment will evoke a response from your soul, abuse will evoke a deeper response from your core, from your spirit. This will be expressed through your soul, but it will be originating from deep inside your spirit.

I have known many people who thought they suffered abuse at the hands of leadership. In few instances do I believe this was actually the case. Through abuse the enemy is going after the God seed planted in you. His plan is to damage you to such an extent that you give up. He is attempting to pervert the message in your heart. However, if you are a child of God, the enemy cannot do this, because your spirit is sealed with the Holy Spirit. If he can convince you of his deceptions, you will actually make these changes yourself. You will actually come to believe the lies you are being told that are contrary to God's Word.

I recall an incident in my life where I was receiving intense pressure to say I believed something that I could not honestly say I believed. There is an integrity we must walk in that keeps us from yielding to the pressure and the control of others to support them in things by saying the Lord has told us something. While man will often pull on you in the hope of receiving confirmation and encouragement, the enemy requires it. He leaves no room for you to reserve opinion. He totally disrespects your free will. He is not satisfied with you simply submitting quietly. He requires you to espouse agreement 100 percent. He requires you to speak it out, which if you cannot do this honestly then you must openly say things that in your heart you do not believe. He knows the God-given power of your words and insists you use them against the Lord's leading. When this temptation occurs, obedience will come at a very high cost—it may be your position, it may be your reputation, it may be your relationship. I can tell you it will be a high cost. To walk as a lover of truth will cost you something, because this is something your enemy does not want you to do and will begin very early in your walk of obedience to get you to compromise. Can you see how this leaves no room for God's gift of free will?

When you are confronted with this type of situation, be very aware that you may be dealing with much more than just the strong personality of a person. If you are being asked to speak on behalf of your precious Lord and you are being strong-armed to say you believe He has said something you cannot honestly say He has spoken to your heart, you are face-to-face with the enemy of your soul and no matter what it costs you, don't yield! Stand faithful. Stand committed to be submitted. Don't say something you know is not the truth! You are in the test of your life. Never yield to the pressure to misrepresent God, no matter what it costs! If you will be faithful to God, respectfully continue to serve and be still, refrain from judging, and leave the matter to the Judge, God will vindicate you in His own way. It may only be in the form of touching your head as you lay it on your pillow, and as the tear hits your cheek, He will let you know how much He loves you and how very proud He is of you. He will call you "friend," and there is no greater gift than to hear those words from the One you serve. You may have to go to your grave never being vindicated on this earth. That must be OK with you, but He will be your defense; He will be your guard. When you are being pressured in this way, the very evil one is attempting to bring you into bondage. Don't do it!

Where spiritual abuse is present there are some common indicators. You may become withdrawn, isolated, confused, or inhibited. These are all words for bondage. Your relationship with the Lord is hindered. You can't seem to hear Him; the channels of communication seem blocked. You may begin to isolate yourself from those who can see what is happening to you, because you do not trust anyone. Isolation is a big indicator. You may become fearful of God, because you have been programmed to believe the Lord will punish you for disagreeing with authority. You may blame yourself and continue to concede to forever demanding changes to operate in a way you are not constructed. The face and eyes are void of joy.

Because of the deep heart cry in all of us, those fallen prey to certain types of spiritual abuse may vehemently defend their abuser for a season, but because the source they are receiving has no life, they will eventually begin to manifest this lack of life in their own lives and behaviors. Eventually they will begin to know something is very wrong, and it is at this point they will begin to try and find their way back. This is the point where many of the external indicators become apparent. Where harsh treatment can drive you toward the Lord, abuse can make you *feel* separated from the Lord. Abuse places something or someone between you and the Lord. Cults always operate in abuse. They seek to break a person, taking control of their will. Abuse always seeks control of a person's will. God always respects a person's will even when it is in opposition to Him. Anyone operating in a manner consistent with Him will do the same. While we are asked to submit our will to the Lord, we are always given the freedom to choose.

While the Lord will many times place you under authority that is harsh, unfair, and difficult, He never asks us to stay under authority where our relationship with Him is being hindered and the enemy is controlling, manipulating, and damaging us spiritually.

Most of us at some time or another think we are being abused. It is similar to the situations we experienced as a child when we knew beyond a doubt our parents hated us and were on the earth to make our lives miserable. As we grow and mature we come to appreciate the reasons behind the methods we once could not understand.

However, there are cases where spiritual abuse is present and help must be sought to escape the situation. If you believe you are in one of these situations, I encourage you to first fall on your face before the Lord, asking Him to forgive you for allowing anyone to have that much control over you. You see, the hard truth of the matter is that we cannot be abused unless we allow someone control over us beyond what is pleasing and acceptable to the Lord. We must fear Him and honor Him above all others. If you will fear the right things, you won't have to worry about fearing the wrong things.

Spiritual abuse can occur when we make our leader our lord. Leaders are to be the Lord's servants over us, but they are not to be our lord. When you give a leader a place intended only for the Lord, you have opened the door for abuse. The Lord is our Comforter, Affirmer, Corrector, Approver, Teacher, Promoter, Source, and the One we are to serve and please. The leader will be used of the Lord to do all of these things. The line we are not to cross is looking to the leader for all these things instead of looking to the Lord and then receiving what He chooses to give us through the leader. When we allow a leader to take this place instead of the Lord, we have made an idol of our leader, opened the door for potential abuse, and at the same time, set the leader up for temptation.

If you have elected to give control of your life to anyone but Jesus, or if you are being pressured to relinquish control to another person, abuse is knocking on your door.

Sometimes we open the door, because we are told this is what we have to do to please the Lord. This is the stumbling block of *self-correction.*

Sometimes we will open the door, because we are curious about the information. This is the stumbling block of *forbidden fruit.*

Sometimes we open the door, because someone has betrayed us. This is the stumbling block of *offense.*

Sometimes we open the door, because we are afraid that if we don't, we will fall from man's favor and not be included in the group. This is the stumbling block of the *fear of man.*

Sometimes we open the door, because we do not trust the Lord with our future and think the person can give us something we need toward promotion. This is self-serving ambition. This is the stumbling block of *fear.*

Sometimes we will open the door, because we don't want to appear overly confident. This is the stumbling block of *false humility.*

Sometimes we open the door, because we are known for how well we open doors. This is trusting in our own ability and the stumbling block of *ability.*

Sometimes we open the door, because we believe our lack of agreement will seem as though we are not a team player. This is the stumbling block of *false unity.*

As you can see, stumbling blocks not overcome in our lives will actually set us up for allowing another person to have a level of control in our lives very displeasing to the Lord. This is really the fertile ground where abuse loves to grow.

Slam the door!

If you are in a situation you believe to be abusive, seek godly counsel. I have to tell you that even though it will be hard and even though you will think it will never be possible, you must learn to trust again, and you must learn to submit to authority. It is your place of safety. This is very difficult to understand for a person who has suffered abuse. You are being asked to assume a position of vulnerability. With the Lord's help you can do what is being asked of you. You will only be able to do this by the grace of God, and He is able and willing to give that grace.

I can hear at this moment the heart cries of some reading this page, "How do I do that?" This is what I believe the Lord would instruct you to do. If you are presently in or suffering the side effects of a past abusive situation (because you either knowingly or unknowingly relinquished control to another in order to gain something that only the Lord should give in His timing), then lay this book down, get on your knees, and ask the Lord to reveal the weakness that allowed someone that level of control in your life.

Outward controls can only attach to a person who has an internal weakness that allows for the connection. Look over the above stumbling blocks, and ask the Lord to reveal to you the open door to your life that allowed the enemy to gain access to you. You will walk through deliverance from spiritual abuse by repenting. This sounds so unfair and as though it cannot be right, because you are the victim. Yes, you are a victim of allowing yourself to operate in a way that was not pleasing to the Lord, and you did it for some reason that is in defiance of His laws. What was done to you was very wrong and never excused by your weakness, but that will be between the other person and the Lord. You have to deal with your part of the situation, and it is going to involve repentance. If you are willing for the Lord to show you where you erred, that act of humility alone will allow for His gift of repentance. You will feel His correction; you will feel His love; you will experience His healing power; and you will be instructed by Him how to prevent this in the future.

The above experience will allow the pain in your soul and the wound on your spirit to be healed. It's called being broken and spilled out. Allow the Lord to touch you right where the problem is; allow Him to take that place of Comforter, Promoter, Corrector, Provider, Friend, Affirmer, and Lover of your soul. When He is the one you are looking to for all of those things, He will many times use others as vessels, but you will never again be vulnerable to others if they do not give this to you, for it is from Him that you receive your strength. This is the place of dependence on the Lord that you want to walk in. This is the place of strength that will absolutely infuriate the devil and will be your only revenge. This is the place of safety the Lord provides.

Maybe you were looking for approval of man above the approval of God. Maybe you were hurt and offended by an injustice and you made decisions in retaliation. Maybe you were afraid of the threats of loss of money, position, respect, or popularity and you did not stand up for what you knew to be pleasing to the Lord. Maybe you had the ability to do a task, and even though the Lord was not releasing you to be the one to do this, you forged ahead anyway just because you could. Maybe you were just so sure you had the answer for the situation and even though you were being resisted you just kept pushing. This is the big one—maybe you wanted to be promoted in your place of ministry and you thought you needed this person to do that for you. Pray and ask the Lord. He will tell you. He will cleanse you, and He will set your feet on high ground.

There are some outstanding Christian counselors who can help you walk the road of healing and restoration. If you feel a need to have additional help, prayerfully seek the counsel the Lord would have for you.

I would like to pray for you right now:

Lord, I pray for my brothers and sisters right now. I thank You for the love and the desire they have in their heart to be pleasing to You and to be used as a vessel for Your purposes. I ask You, Lord, to bring to their remembrance the areas they compromised to gain anything from anyone other than You. I ask, Lord, for a gift of repentance to fall on them at this moment, that they would feel Your love, they would hear Your instruction, and they would be set free from every chain that has been placed on them to bind them and separate them from You. Lord, I pray You will touch them from the tops of their heads to the tips of their toes with the oil of Your presence. I pray they would feel Your healing and cleansing power. I bind every thought of condemnation and shame, and I set at liberty their bruised hearts. They were made to serve You, worship You, and love You, and I set them free to do that completely. I speak clarity of mind and cleansing of their soul from all of the bondage of confusion. I ask they rest in the knowledge of Your goodness, and Your all-knowing position. I pray they would enter into a rest in You and a peace that passes all understanding. I bind every lying thought that would try to tell them they have not been healed and cleansed, and I ask for total deliverance from all deception. Lord, I pray their trust level in You would exceed any doubt that would ever again steer them away from trusting You. I ask this all in the authority of the name of Jesus. Let it be done!

That prayer carries power—life-altering, yoke-destroying power, not because of me, but simply because it is the Father's heart for all of His children. He loves us, and He has a way of wiping away dirt and grime from our souls that we have picked up over our journey. He brings us into the truth of His Word not to condemn us but to deliver us from all unrighteousness. Take a deep breath, release all the junk, receive His forgiveness and restoration, and go and sin no more.

There will be many opportunities for you to be tempted, especially over the next few days, to think nothing happened here and that you are really not free. This will be your opportunity to have life and death set before you and to choose life. When the thoughts come in, when you hear that accusers voice, immediately reject the thought and come into agreement with the promise that He whom the Son has set free is free indeed. (See John 8:36.) The truth is you were set free two thousand years ago; you just did not appropriate it in your life in this area. The enemy lied to you and you believed him. His is a liar. Never listen. When you feel the battle, begin to pray a prayer over yourself, knowing it is the power in the name of Jesus that drives back all oppression. Never agree with the enemy. Stand in the faith that the Lord has delivered you from all evil and purpose in your heart to walk it out daily. Trust Him!

For all others who feel so misunderstood, I hope you now have differentiated between harsh treatment, which the Lord clearly expects you to endure, and abuse. The message in the case of abuse is get out! In the case of harsh and unfair treatment, stand faithful. The Lord loves you very much. Seek Him, be obedient to His instructions, and you will be in the right place at the right time for His purposes.

Now, go back to the front of this chapter and read the Scripture reference at the top. Remember that all scripture is given for your edification and is never intended by the Lord to condemn His children (2 Tim. 3:16). It may correct you, and it may convict you, because the Lord corrects those who are His, but it is not given to condemn you!

Carryover Thoughts

- It is the Lord who is to be our Promoter, Affirmer, Developer, and Protector. He alone is the One we are to look to for approval, advancement, and promotion.
- Looking to anyone else for approval, advancement, and promotion will set us up for disappointment, frustration, delay, and maybe abuse.

Chapter 11

THE STONE OF STUMBLING—THE FINAL HURDLE

> And the Scriptures also say, "He is the stone that makes people stumble, the rock that will make them fall"
>
> —1 Peter 2:8

In a previous chapter we discussed the mentoring relationship between Elijah and Elisha. The point made in that story was that although Elisha did all the right things to stay in right relationship with his leader, those necessary acts of obedience were essentially stepping stones to position him to overcome the final hurdle to receiving what was in his heart to have. Elisha admired and respected his mentor. The power and presence of the Lord that operated through Elijah was something Elisha wanted to have. He didn't just want the same level of power; he wanted a double portion of that power. Elisha had to know and understand God's ways to the point that he would accurately interpret the final events that occurred when Elijah was taken away by the horses and chariots of fire. If he could do this, he would be entrusted with what he desired. If he could not, he would walk away without the portion he was seeking. This is such a parallel story to our walking in all the power and authority the Lord has destined for us to have.

The stumbling blocks mentioned to this point are human frailties not consistent with God's nature. To overcome these tendencies we must submit our lives to Him and become more like Him through intimate fellowship and submission to His ways. These stumbling blocks are the nature of Adam, which is the nature of Satan. We must recognize them, resist them, overcome them, and walk free of their effect in our lives by the work of the cross.

There is another stone we must contend with. We must embrace this stone, allow ourselves to be crushed by this stone, and build our lives on this stone. (See Ps. 62:7.) Our Jesus is the "stone of stumbling." If we do not understand our Savior, and if we do not know Him intimately, we will not recognize Him, and He will become an offense to us. He is the "stone of stumbling," and to stumble over this stone is the last thing we ever want to do. His words are spirit and life, and we must hear them and know Him in spirit. Just as Elisha had to see what God was doing in the spirit, so we must do the same if He is to entrust to us greater dimensions of His power and authority. Our relationship with Him is by the spirit, and while our heads interpret Him, it is not our head that recognizes and communes with Him. We know Him in our heart, we know Him by the spirit, and we recognize Him by the spirit. Many of the precious things He will say and do, if we hear them with our heads and try and understand them with our natural minds, will sound very offensive. How is this so?

In chapter 7 of the Gospel of Luke we have the situation where John the Baptist is in the dungeon of a prison. He is hours away from having his head cut from his body and delivered on a platter to an evil woman who did not like the truth he spoke. This is a man who leaped in his mother's womb when Mary announced to Elizabeth that she was pregnant with the Messiah. This was the man who as a young boy chose the strictest of paths to serving God. He knew Jesus, he was the one who baptized Jesus, and he had even stated that he was not worthy to buckle the sandals Jesus wore. In his final hours as he was obviously contemplating his life, he sent one of his disciples to ask Jesus a question. He wanted to know if Jesus was the Messiah or should they look for another. It appears this question was based on the obvious comparison of the two lives of John and Jesus. John and his disciples would fast and drink no wine. Jesus and His disciples did not fast and drank wine. Jesus associated with those who were considered outcasts and misfits. And now, after serving the Lord all his life, he finds himself imprisoned, accused, beaten, hated, and moments from losing his life because he refused to compromise the truth. I'm sure John was in a state of extreme discouragement. Everything he believed to be true was being questioned. Jesus' answer to John's question was minimal at best. He simply told John's disciple to go back and tell him of the miracles he had seen and punctuated the message with the statement, "God blesses those who are not offended by me" (Matt. 11:6).

Jesus knew the battle raging in John's mind. He knew John's preconceived expectations had not been met, and He knew that John was being tempted to be offended by Him. Those things in the life of Jesus that did not match up with John's theology were potential stumbling blocks to John believing Jesus was who He said He was. How easy it would have been for Jesus to eliminate all doubt for John. And yet, He did not do that. He simply reminded Him of the signs that pointed to His identity. It was only after John's disciple was out of earshot that Jesus went on to tell those around Him that John was the greatest of all the prophets. John died not being given the luxury of natural evidence that Jesus was who He said He was. He died having to know and recognize Jesus by the spirit and not by natural signs. He could have stumbled, but he did not!

Jesus will never meet all of our preconceived expectations. He will never perfectly line up with our theology. If we require this, we will stumble at His ways. We will become offended and we will walk away. We may not walk away from all we know of Him, but we will walk away from that part we do not understand. When we embrace all of Him is when we will begin to walk in a place of intimacy few find. His relationship with each of us is personal and it is private. How we communicate and respond to Him may be very different than another, but it should never be limited to just what we are comfortable with experiencing. We are as close to Him as we want to be.

We must also be sensitive to how we influence others in the development of their relationship or how we respond to the relationship they have. While there are certain things we know by Scripture that are not true, many of the different styles of expression that we do not understand are scripturally modeled. While I would not want to shave my head and lay on my side for a year, if I saw someone doing something that odd, I have learned to reserve judgment. This is something the prophet Ezekiel felt the need to do in accordance with an instruction from God. I may be tempted to think the person is a nut. I may think they have missed God's instruction; but I would still reserve my opinion. I would pray for them and ask God for the grace to be quiet and just see. While that is a very extreme example, it is a good one to illustrate how very odd behavior is modeled in the Word we believe to be 100 percent inspired by God.

I am very uncomfortable when churches have foot-washing services. It is simply an uncomfortable situation for me. If a church decides to have such a ceremony, I'm not touching it. I will not risk being offended by my Jesus. It may not be Him—it may—but the bottom line is no one is going to get hurt and there may be something very powerful that the Lord can do through that type of exercise. Jesus made mud pies with spit and healed blind eyes. He turned tables over and threw a tantrum in the temple. He insulted people. All of these things fall a bit outside what we may expect from the man with the lamb around His neck and the staff in His hand. We do not have Him all figured out, and we need to reserve judgment on things we may not understand.

As Jesus walked the earth and made disciples there came a day of great testing for some of those who followed Him. John tells the story in the sixth chapter of his Gospel. Jesus was addressing many of His followers, and His words were much too strong for them to digest. Jesus clearly stretched people to hear Him by the spirit, to teach them to know Him, and to communicate in spirit and in truth. He would use metaphors for the purpose of making His point, and it was that picture that would open their ears to hear. Oftentimes Jesus said, "Anyone who is willing to hear should listen and understand" (Matt. 11:15). That statement must have been frustrating for those who could not hear what He was saying by the spirit. But it also was a loving move on His part, because it put them on notice that if they did not have understanding, they needed to search for understanding. Jesus would press people to labor to understand.

On this day Jesus told them He was the Bread of Life and that they must eat His flesh and drink His blood. To hear this in the natural and not by the spirit is very grotesque to say the least. The story goes on to say that many were offended and many walked away that day not able to follow Him. They were offended; they stumbled on the "stone of stumbling." They stumbled because they were too naturally minded and not able to hear in the spiritual context what Jesus was saying. They lacked faith, knowledge, and understanding. Hopefully, many of those who stumbled were able to be taught and nurtured and at a later time were able to return to their commitment to follow Jesus.

There is a position of humility that allows for us to realize that no matter how fully we think we know something, no matter how fully we think we understand something, there is a chance we may not have all the pieces of the puzzle. In those times when we don't understand, it is best to simply reserve opinion and trust God to give us understanding in His timing.

One of the most liberating moments of my life was the day I realized I didn't have to have an opinion. That was simply an amazing concept for me. Many of us are much like Peter in our early days as a fervent and bold disciple. We come to know the Lord and begin to learn of His ways, and just like the little kid who thinks his daddy is the biggest, toughest, and best, we think everything we have been taught is 100 percent accurate and 100 percent complete. It is in those times we act much like Peter. We cut off ears, and we rebuke the Lord. Our natural nature is breaking forth in all directions, and we think we are on a mission for God! His patience is wonderful, but there is much power in realizing that you don't have to have an opinion. You can rest in the place of, "I don't know." The Lord gives us much liberty to take that route. Let's look further at the story.

After so many had walked away, Jesus turned to His twelve disciples and asked, "Are you going to leave, too?" (John 6:67). Their response was a smart one. They didn't seem certain how to interpret what He had said, but they were smart enough to reserve judgment. They knew enough to not walk away. Peter replied, "Lord, to whom would we go? You alone have the words that give eternal life" (John 6:68). In my life, when this has happened, although it may take years, the time comes that the Lord brings understanding. He is the best teacher. When He left His disciples He told them that He had much to say to them but they would not be able to understand it at that time. Be patient and know that as you are able to hear. The Lord will bring what you need to gain the knowledge and understanding you want.

To not understand but to reserve opinion is a place of safety. It is an act of respect and it will serve you well by preserving relationships. To not understand and to walk away will limit you, but in keeping with the Lord's promise to be patient with us, His arms are always open for our return.

There is, however, a deeper degree of distain that can put us at odds with the God we serve. Let's look at 2 Samuel 6.

David was the king of Israel and was married to a beautiful woman by the name of Michal who was the daughter of King Saul. Michal loved David very much. David loved Michal, but he also loved the Lord with all his heart. He was a man after God's heart, and he was a man God trusted to lead His people with His heart. On this special day, the ark of the covenant was being brought into the City of David. David, in his unabashed delight, danced before the Lord with all his might, jumping and leaping as the ark was entering the city. As he was expressing his joy before the Lord, Michal looked out her window. As she looked upon him "she was filled with contempt for him" (v. 16). As David approached his home, Michal came out to meet him, and she addressed him with disgust. She was offended and disgusted by the expression of joy and love David exhibited toward the Lord. She insulted him and she ridiculed him. She was offended by his love and relationship with the Lord, and she spoke to him in a manner that would seem to try to make him ashamed of what he had done. David was not ashamed, and he retorted. Michal was barren from that point on all the days of her life. She despised the life that was free flowing from David. She hated what she saw, she spoke against it, and consequently she was denied the natural gift of bringing life into the world.

When we see what we consider to be an extreme expression of joy or some other emotion toward the Lord that we may not be comfortable with, our ability to identify with the expression does not substantiate or unsubstantiated its validity. While we may not be able to identify with the expression, and while we certainly should not feel pressure to model the expression, we must, out of respect for our brothers and sisters, esteem them and their love for their Lord. Our expressions of displeasure, in an attempt to make people like us, can put us in the position of being denied the gift of carrying and giving the life of God.

To bring balance to this perspective, I believe expressions should certainly be at appropriate times and not a source of complete distraction and confusion. Leadership often establishes boundaries for expression in the general assembly. This is often times viewed as too restrictive by some who want no constraints. While we should all be given the freedom to express ourselves freely to the Lord, we should all respect the guidelines set forth by the leadership in open gatherings. This insures order and eliminates confusion. There is a great story that addresses this guideline.

Years ago, in the 1950s, there lived a dynamic evangelist by the name of Mordecai Ham. Mordecai was a fiery Baptist tent evangelist who led many lost souls to Christ. One such person was a young man by the name of Billy Graham. He was saved at one of Mordecai's tent revivals. Mordecai would go into towns and create such a stir that he would receive death threats attempting to drive him out of town. He hated alcohol with a passion, and he loved God with an even greater passion. His fiery preaching style would melt the hardest of hearts and literally hundreds would walk to the altar at the end of his sermons. There were actually times when the local bars would be almost empty, because so many of the local people were being saved and delivered from the addiction to alcohol.

About the same time as Mordecai was gaining great popularity and people were being saved in great numbers in his meetings, there was another movement sweeping the country called the Charismatic Renewal Movement. People in this group were also being saved and experiencing intimacy with the Lord through the ministry of the Holy Spirit. Some of these people began coming to Mordecai's services and in their zeal they would speak loudly in tongues at various times during the meeting. This was very distracting, and they were asked to be quiet. In their fervor and their belief that this was something God wanted them to do, they continued in their activity. Mordecai did not have a problem with their speaking in tongues; he had a problem with their distracting his service and interfering with his sermon. It finally became such a problem that he had to refuse to allow them to come to the service. What a sad story! They were very much out of order and their rebellion to the God-established authority brought great division. They did not respect the minister the Lord had put in charge. While we are not to devalue what others are experiencing in the Lord, which Mordecai certainly did not, we are also not to push our ways on others. The decision on their part to disrespect Mordecai brought a great divide in the church that never had to be there. Had they respected the leader, they may have been instrumental to introducing their experiences to others. However, because they chose to be offended at Mordecai's authority, authority given by Jesus, they were actually offended at Jesus all the while thinking they were being His mouthpiece. Always remember, the Holy Spirit does not interrupt the Holy Spirit!

"If you think you are standing strong, be careful, for you, too, may fall into the same sin" (1 Cor. 10:12). It matters not one bit where we fall on the chart in experience and maturity. Any of us can fall from any point. While we may be tempted to think that falling in the beginning of our walk with the Lord is more common, this scripture clearly indicates this is not true. Notice it says that we are in danger of falling when we "think" we stand. When we start out in our relationship with the Lord, we know we're weak. As we grow and develop, we may begin to think we are standing because we have become strong. It is when we are trusting in our own strength and ability that we are most susceptible to a fall. To continue to spend precious time with the one we serve, to continue to seek Him in all our decisions, will keep us in a place of safety and His rock will not trip us. Desperate dependence on the one we serve is the greatest sign of a mature and submitted heart. It is when we move out from under His hand of guidance that we lose our sensitivity to His spirit and therefore risk being offended by what is really Him!

> But the Jews, who tried so hard to get right with God by keeping the law, never succeeded. Why not? Because they were trying to get right with God by keeping the law and being good instead of by depending on faith. They stumbled over the great rock in their path. God warned them of this in the Scriptures when he said, "I am placing a stone in Jerusalem that causes people to stumble, and a rock that makes them fall. But anyone who believes in him will not be disappointed."
>
> —Romans 9:31–33

Believing in Jesus is more than an initial decision. Believing in Jesus is maintaining, no matter how long we have walked with Him, a dependence on His leading and a submission to His lordship. When we acknowledge Him in all our ways He will direct our path. (See Prov. 3:6.)

> But watch out, you who live in your own light and warm yourselves by your own fires. This is the reward you will receive from me: You will soon lie down in great torment.
>
> —Isaiah 50:11

The more we know Him, the more we will realize our need for His constant protection in our lives. We must know Him, talk with Him, and understand Him by the spirit, not with our natural understanding. If we walk in our natural understanding according to our natural tendencies, we will trip over the "stone of stumbling." The things of God cannot be discerned or understood by the natural mind. They are foolishness to the natural mind. (See 1 Cor. 2:14.)

This is a good time to reflect on the circumstances we discussed surrounding Elisha and how he overcame the distractions of the "sons of the prophets." It is a good time to look over your life and identify the "sons of the prophets" that are in your life and how you may be listening to their warnings. We must discern who is in our lives and why they are there. Remember, these were serious students. They were diligent to study and to be mentored by the best of the day. What they were saying to Elisha was factual. They were sincere, educated, and committed. They were very wrong in their interpretation, because they viewed the situation with natural eyes and natural understanding. Had Elisha listened to them, not only would he not have received his promotion, he would have wasted his time roaming about the land looking for a man who could not be found!

I pray we all, like Elisha, scale this hurdle like an Olympic runner!

Carryover Thoughts

- We will never have our Lord completely figured out on this earth.
- Knowledge is available for the taking.
- Wisdom is freely given to those who ask.
- Understanding comes as we learn through our experiences or the experiences of others.
- You must know, by the spirit, who is in your life and why!

CHAPTER 12

RESOLVE—THE FIXED AND TRUSTING HEART

> Because the Sovereign LORD helps me, I will not be dismayed. Therefore, I have set my face like a stone, determined to do his will. And I know that I will triumph. He who gives me justice is near. Who will dare to oppose me now? Where are my enemies? Let them appear! See, the Sovereign LORD is on my side! Who will declare me guilty? All my enemies will be destroyed like old clothes that have been eaten by moths!
>
> —ISAIAH 50:7–9

THERE COMES A time for all of us when we must begin to live what we proclaim. To desire to walk in the ways of the almighty God, to walk in His awesome power, and to do the works He did, requires resolve. It requires a yielding to His lordship. It requires becoming a bondservant of the Most High God. A bondservant is a servant by choice. There is freedom to leave, to walk away, and to go our own way. There is freedom to stay and fulfill all the things we have expressed a desire to fulfill. The choice is yours. You can decide to give the Lord the reigns of your life, or you can decide to continue to operate in some level of control. The choice is yours; the Lord will respect your decision.

To give the Lord the reigns of your life requires you to walk in obedience to His ways and His Word. It requires you to lay down your right to be right. It requires you to deny your carnal desires interfering with His desires.

Every stumbling block exposed in the previous chapters can only cause you to stumble if you give into the carnal nature we are called to crucify. You must purpose in your heart it is now time to forget about yourself and concentrate on Him. We sing the songs, close our eyes, and mouth all the right words only to walk in bondage to thinking of ourselves—what we want, what we need, what others are doing to us, what others are getting, and how others are being blessed. We stand in a place of ungratefulness, envy consuming our soul. This must not be. This cannot be if we are to walk in the place of servanthood to our God. God's generals are God's servants.

It can no longer be that we carelessly handle information from the tree of the knowledge of good and evil. The power the Lord has entrusted to His children must be used with respect. It must be used in obedience to His Spirit. Information gathered must be handled in obedience to the Lord. You are not to be alive; it is He who is alive in you and you no longer have the right to handle information with your own understanding.

It can no longer be that we become easily offended by the actions of others. This is not an option to the servant of the Lord. Offense has one purpose and one purpose only—to cause division within the body of Christ. This cannot be allowed. It must be stopped, and it starts with you and me.

It can no longer be that we care more for what man thinks than what the Lord thinks. We strive harder to please man than to please the Lord. He is the only One we should be desperate to please. As we please Him we will oftentimes please others. We will oftentimes not. It depends on the motives of those around us, but our desire must be to please the Lord and to love Him with all our hearts.

It can no longer be that we alter our God-ordained destiny for fear we will suffer persecution, loss, and suffering. We are called to lay our lives down for our Lord. We must have a resolve of heart to do what we are called to do no matter what the cost.

It can no longer be that we are self-conscious and in fear of someone thinking we are full of pride, because we have an awesome confidence in our God. We must no longer hide our candle under a bushel, being so conscious of our actions. We can no longer tolerate behavior from others that hinders the advancement of the troops, because we do not want to appear bossy and controlling. Those appointed must take the responsibility delegated by Jesus, operate in His love, and begin to train and position troops. To forbear childish behavior from those who are no longer children will hold God's people in bondage and delay the maturing process. It fosters strife and feeds attitudes of rebellion, self-pity, and selfishness. An undisciplined child is a miserable child. An undisciplined child is a child that will never fulfill their destiny. An undisciplined child will make an undisciplined soldier and will get the entire company of soldiers killed because of their foolishness. Leadership that does not discipline God's children does not love God's children. It is not true love that allows a person to continue in a dysfunction that is altering their life plan and therefore the lives of those around them.

Those called must begin to equip the saints for the work of the ministry. We must have a focus of the power and the realness of our God where we no longer think of the consequences of what others will perceive but walk in a desperate dependence on His leading, and then do it! There is a battle to be fought and a victory to be celebrated. Trained warriors know how to fight and win.

It can no longer be that we assume control of the God-given abilities the Lord has placed in us for His purposes. This is *His* battle and *His* plan, and it must be run according to *His* will. I believe the day is very soon coming when what we say must be what we mean, or the Holy Spirit will judge us as lying against Him. God gives us the choice to do whatever it is we desire to do; the action He will not tolerate is our portraying one thing while doing another.

In Acts 4–5 there is a story I would like for us to review. At the time this story occurred, the church was growing in strength and numbers. People were coming into the knowledge of the truth. They were beginning to operate in the principles taught by Jesus and experience God's blessing as a result of their obedience.

In this story some of the believers had been selling portions of their property and bringing all of the money into the church to be divided among those in need. Because of this there was no poverty found among them. A couple by the name of Ananias and Sapphira sold some land but conspired privately to hold back a portion of the proceeds, giving only a portion to the church. First Ananias came before the church, presented the money, and stated it is all of the proceeds from his land. The apostle Peter's asked him why he lied to the Holy Spirit. (See Acts 4:3.) As soon as those words were spoken, Ananias fell dead. About three hours later Ananias's wife, Sapphira, arrived, unaware of the fate of her husband. Peter asked her, "Was this the price you and your husband received from your land?" She replied "Yes" (v. 8). Peter again exposed the deception and she fell dead as well. Not a good day for two people who were giving an offering to the church.

While we may read this story and surmise their error was not giving all of the money from the land, is that accurate? Peter explained to Sapphira that is was their right to sell or not sell the land, and it was their right to keep all or a part of the money. They had the liberty to keep all they earned; they chose to keep back a portion. However, rather than be forthright and honest, they agreed to lie about the portion kept back. While they wanted to keep back a portion for themselves, they wanted the people to think they were giving all they received. The intolerable action was their misrepresentation before the people of God, not that they wanted to keep a portion of the proceeds. They lied to the Holy Spirit! It cost them their lives. Whatever it is you are saying must be true. He does not demand we be perfect. He does not demand we not make mistakes, but He absolutely requires our honesty when we stand before others and testify of our deeds. If you are saying you have committed to the Lord the abilities He has given you, then He must be given lordship over all you have. You must do what it is you are saying.

It can no longer be that we compromise the power of the gospel for the sake of no conflict, thinking this to be unity. Unity does not mean conflict will not exist. Unity means in the face of conflict common goals are accomplished. It means the persons involved love the Lord to such a degree that they are willing to forbear the frailties of others for the common good of all. It means the body has matured to the point that there is mutual respect even when there is not complete understanding. It means we have grown beyond not thinking more highly of ourselves than we should. It means our life is not our own. It has been paid for by the price of Christ's blood. It means we are obedient to find our place, get in our place, stay in our place, and do what it is the Lord is asking us to do. It means we lay down our need to be known and affirmed by anyone except the Lord. Unity will ensure we get the job done we have all been wanting to see done. Unity is giving the Lord total control. Because He is complete unity, He understands what needs to be done, and He really is able to accomplish it through us if we will just yield.

It can no longer be that we make all the decisions concerning our ministries and ourselves. The Lord is the Lord. This sounds like an unnecessary statement to make, but the truth is that He is not the Lord in many lives and in many ministries. He is rather expected to show up and bless what man has made. His long-suffering and mercy is unfathomable.

The Lord will have an army. It is His choice who is placed in the positions required. We can no longer continue to place people on the basis of some natural understanding and criteria God does not use. We must mature to the point we are able to know those who labor among us by the spirit. This is done by knowing our Lord Jesus. By knowing Him, we will begin to recognize Him in others. We must respect His appointments and we must submit to the authority He has placed over us. We must respect the persons He has assigned to be linked with us, and we must respect the method He chooses for accomplishing the goals He sets. It is all His plan, all His methods, and all His decisions. We are to be obedient to the Lord's directives.

We know our Commander in Chief is the Captain of the host. He is the Boss. He will have control. He will take over. Whether you are called to serve on air, land, or sea, it is of utmost importance you find your place, get in your place, and stay in your place. Generals are appointed by the Lord. They must take their place and the Lord will begin to send those linked to their assignment. The kingdom of God is an upside-down kingdom; generals will be on the bottom. They are the ones who are called to serve others the most. The army will build on the foundation of Jesus and His chosen generals. Layer upon layer will be formed until we all come into the unity of the faith.

For such a time as this the Lord has chosen to allow you to be alive on the earth. It is truly to be the great and dreadful day of the Lord. It will be great for the Lord and His people and dreadful for the enemy and those who have chosen to go his way. Let this heart of a warrior be in you. It is His heart; it is His ability; it is His strength. If you desire to fulfill your God-ordained destiny, then you have been called. If you desire to be chosen and are willing to allow the Lord to remove what needs to be removed and adjust what needs to be adjusted, so you will be ready for battle. He is ready at this moment to put you on the path required to launch you into your next season. If you are feeling His presence, if you are sensing His drawing, or if you are not sensing anything but want to pray the following prayer, submit. I believe this prayer will carry the life of God and I believe He will touch you and begin to prepare you for the service He has ordained.

> *Father, in the name of Jesus I come to You broken of all my desires, all my needs, all my dreams, and all my plans. I lay this day on Your altar—every plan, every fear, every failure, every offense, every ability, every piece of knowledge, every gift, every accomplishment, every commitment, and everything I ever hoped to be. I lay it all on the altar today, giving to You all I have and asking You to give to me that which You have and desire for me to have this day. I submit to Your lordship over my life, money, possessions, dreams, and plans. I submit to Your lordship in my life. I ask You, Lord, to remind me of the instructions I have failed to follow. I ask You to place back in my hands those things You desire I continue. This is a new day, and this is the beginning of my walk as a servant of You, Lord. I give You my life; I give you my dreams; I give you the call on my life and ask You to show me what it is I am to do this day. Flush my vessel, Lord, and bring me into a relationship with You that is more intimate every day. Give me eyes to see and ears to hear what is being said by Your Spirit every day. I ask You, Lord, to show me my place, give me my assignment, and grant me the grace to stay within my assignment. Above all, I want to know You, I want to serve You, and I want to please You. Forgive me for leaning to my own understanding, and help me to acknowledge You in all of my ways from this day forward. Amen!*

I believe with all my heart that if you prayed the above prayer, the Lord has already launched you into a new depth of service. I know He desires to do all you have asked of Him. He loves you and wants nothing more than for you to walk in all He has called you to be. Your decision to serve Him must have no conditions. You must trust Him in all situations. To do this, you must know Him intimately.

There are many promises the Lord has given us in His Word. He promises to be faithful, never to leave us, never to forsake us, to give us grace in our time of need, to be our Comforter and our Counselor, our Provider, Healer, and Redeemer. He has also assured us we will suffer tribulation and persecution. Tribulation is the circumstances in our lives that come to wear us down; persecution comes at the hand of people. We have tribulation in circumstances and persecution from people.

The Lord has said if we are to reign with Him we will also suffer with Him. We will suffer as His Spirit in us grieves as we walk in obedience to His instructions and are rejected by those He so desires to help. When you feel the Lord's heart you will feel His longing to serve His people and you will feel His suffering. It is not yours; it is His. You are being allowed to share in His suffering. Never complain, for it is an honor.

You must purpose in your heart that no matter how circumstances appear you will maintain your belief that the Lord is just and His Word is true. You must be prepared to never see the fruition of a promise in your lifetime, trusting it will come to pass. There can be no conditions on our service to the Lord. We do not have the ability to always understand. His ways truly are higher than our ways. If you are serving Him with obedience, be content in whatever circumstances exist. As you yield to His ways, He will give you His heart and, when you have His heart, you will be equipped with His power.

Whenever your heel is bleeding, whenever you have taken a blow because of your stand for Christ, know you have crushed a head. While the enemy may strike you in the heel because of his hate for Jesus, because he is the enemy of God it will result in his head being crushed. (See Gen. 3:15.) Do not look at your bruised heel, but rather look at the head you have crushed. We spend so much of our time whining over and nursing our bruised heel, all the while never seeing the attacks of the enemy we were allowed to halt. Sit at the feet of Jesus. Climb in His lap. He will whisper the plans and the purposes of circumstances in your ear. He will give you understanding if you will seek understanding. It will empower you to not notice what otherwise would be interpreted as suffering. He will say, "Forget that little scratch on your heel. Look over here at this crushed head." When He allows you to see what was actually accomplished in a situation, your battle scar will become a jewel in your crown and you will shout with a shout of triumph!

I too have prayed the prayer on page 185. I may never know you this side of heaven, but you are my brother or you are my sister, and, if we are in our places of assignment, we are in unity. My prayer for you is that you will have a resolve of heart, committed and submitted to the Lord of all, and that your uniform is tailored and a perfect fit. I pray that you will love the Lord with an unconditional love only He can give you that will in turn empower your heart to be fixed and prepared for commitment to service in the face of adversity. I pray that you will be prepared, purposed, focused, and aimed to fulfill all the Lord has destined you to fulfill, for such a time as this, to the glory of our precious Lord and Savior, Jesus!

A Final Word

Be strong with the Lord's mighty power. Put on all of God's armor so that you will be able to stand firm against all strategies and tricks of the Devil. For we are not fighting against people made of flesh and blood, but against the evil rulers and authorities of the unseen world, against those mighty powers of darkness who rule this world, and against wicked spirits in the heavenly realms. Use every piece of God's armor to resist the enemy in the time of evil, so that after the battle you will still be standing firm.

—EPHESIANS 6: 10–13

NOTES

Chapter 2

The Stumbling Block of Self-Correction

1. Sam Goldaper, *New York Times Obituary*, http:/www.bigbluehistory.net/bb/statistics/coaches/Adolph_Rupp.html (accessed 2/23/07).

For more information and to contact the author,
go to www.narrowgateministry.org.